The
New
Evangelical
Theology

The
New
Evangelical
Theology

Millard Erickson

Fleming H. Revell Company
Westwood, New Jersey

Scripture quotations identified as KJV in this publication are from the *King James Version of the Bible*.

Scripture quotations identified as RSV in this publication are from *The Revised Standard Version of the Bible*, copyright 1946 and 1952.

To
GINNY

Preface

The December 20, 1963, issue of *Time* magazine carried an article in its religion section entitled "The Evangelical Undertow." It spoke of a "hard-to-map third stream in American Protestantism, running midway between the simplistic fundamentalism . . . and the sophisticated faith espoused by a majority of the nation's best-known theologians and denominational leaders." The gist of the article was that there is a strong and growing conservative element that is becoming intellectually respectable, and that it must be reckoned with.

The author of this book is of the conviction that this movement is indeed a significant factor in the contemporary Protestant theological scene. He is further convinced that this theology, best known as "The New Evangelicalism," has not been sufficiently analyzed and assessed. It is therefore his concern to draw together and expound the history and the thought of this new theological movement.

The movement is indeed hard to map, and he has therefore concentrated on the thought of a few men who are clearly identified with this reaction against fundamentalism:

Harold Ockenga, Carl Henry, Billy Graham, Bernard Ramm, Vernon Grounds, and the late Edward Carnell. The thought of others is drawn on, but less extensively. A different aspect of the life and thought of the new evangelicalism is dealt with in each chapter.

During the years from approximately 1910 to 1930 conservative and liberal Christians were engaged in a sharp and sometimes bitter conflict known as the "Fundamentalist-Modernist Controversy." Following the controversy, each group withdrew from the other; dialogue ceased. In the past two decades, due in part to the effort of the new evangelicals, there has been the beginning of resumption of such theological interchange. This book is put forth with the hope that it will prove of value to all elements of the theological universe. It has been written not only for the theologian and minister, but also for the informed layman, and the style reflects that objective. For those desiring to investigate the subject more thoroughly, a fairly extensive bibliography is included.

I wish to thank the administration of Wheaton College for a research grant during the summer of 1966, and for providing special facilities for research and writing. I appreciate the helpful suggestions made by many different persons regarding the contents. I am particularly indebted to Dr. William Hordern, president of Lutheran Theological Seminary, Saskatoon, Canada. As my advisor in the doctoral program at Northwestern University, he encouraged me to publish on this subject, and as a sympathetic student of the movement, offered valuable insights. Portions of earlier drafts were read and evaluated by Dr. Roger Blackwell of Ohio State University, from the standpoint of a layman, and Rev. David Olson of Harvest Publications, from the perspective of an editor. Among my colleagues at Wheaton College, Dr. Morris Inch read the entire manuscript in its penultimate form and made several constructive comments, and Dr. Samuel Schultz shared procedural suggestions. My teaching assistants, Norman Kapp, Edwin Brainerd, and Paul Engle, helped with research and clerical detail.

More than any other person, however, my wife Virginia has made the writing of this book possible. Not only did she painstakingly type each draft and assist with matters of style, but her faith, hope, and love were a constant encouragement to me.

MILLARD ERICKSON

Wheaton, Illinois

Contents

I

The Historical Development

The year is 1946. The war has ended. Americans, for so long preoccupied with the international scene, are again beginning to think about domestic affairs. Long-range planning, which has seemed rather irrelevant, again occupies men's thought. The church is carefully examining itself in terms of its needs, resources, and opportunities.

In the heart of metropolitan Boston, a man sits in his study in a large church, deep in reflection. Particularly sensitive to the religious situation in New England, he sees powerful blocs or forces at work: liberalism, Roman Catholicism, and Unitarianism. All of these are competing for the position of ascendancy and influence in society. Though none of these groups has the true solution to man's needs, each is emphatically and persuasively pressing its claim.

This man is Dr. Harold Ockenga, pastor of the historic Park Street Church. He is a conservative, one who holds and advocates the "fundamentals" of the faith. This evangelical Christianity he believes to be true and to be the ultimate solution to man's spiritual, moral, and social needs. Yet it is not really making that impact upon America. "Why?" he asks himself as he paces the floor of his study. To him, evangelical Christianity has neglected a basic part of its heritage. Whereas conservative Christianity had traditionally concerned itself with the application of the gospel message to social problems, contemporary fundamentalism has tended to ignore this dimension of its message, resulting in its irrelevance in the thinking of many people.

Just a few miles away from Park Street Church, a twenty-seven-year-old graduate student is studying in the library of the Harvard University Divinity School. He, too, is a conservative Christian by background and by conviction. He also is uneasy about the status of fundamentalism. Examining the rows of books on reserve for courses in the divinity school, he can find scarcely a work by a conservative. In his classes, references to the contribution of conservative theologians are very rare. Conservative theology is not really a live option for theologians and students at an institution such as Harvard, and for good reason. Since the times of such intellectual and literary giants as James Orr, Benjamin Warfield, and J. Gresham Machen, conservative scholarship has declined. This young man, Edward Carnell, hears no effective voice sounding forth its message.

In the midwest, a seminary professor strolls along a boulevard in Chicago, conversing with one of his colleagues. They are concerned about the frame of mind or spirit which fundamentalism seems to have assumed. Having begun as a reaction against theological deviation, it has become increasingly negative in character. Once concerned to separate itself from error in doctrine and life, it has become divisive. A harsh temperament, a spirit of loveless-ness and strife seem to dominate the movement. The theo-logical debate with modernism has in many cases degen-erated into attacks upon personalities and organizations. Thus, unfortunately, conservatism in theology has come to be associated in many persons' minds with an unlovely spirit, and is avoided by many. The man is Carl F. H. Henry, professor of philosophy of religion at Northern Bap-tist Seminary.

Each of these men, painfully aware of these shortcom-ings of fundamentalism, is also nonetheless convinced that the fundamentalist position most nearly approximates theo-logical truth. Yet it seems to them that fundamentalism is receiving a poor hearing because it is not being properly presented. The efforts of its recent proponents have done more to harm its influence than to strengthen, extend, and enhance it.

Yet they are not pessimistic. A note of hope is present in their minds and hearts. Since fundamentalism does embody truth, is it not possible to make a more adequate case for it? Could not the essential truth of its message be stated and defended with academic competence, in an irenic spirit, and with a due concern for the social implications of its ethical thrust? These men, initially developing their thought quite independently of one another, became the nucleus of just such a "new evangelicalism" within American Protestant-ism. This development in American conservative theology has grown in vigor and is today a force to be reckoned with.

The way in which a plant develops is very much affected

by the soil in which it grows. The same is true of a theology. Theology is dynamic. It stems from the dialogue and inter-action of different ideas, events, and men. New forms of thought arise in response to demands of history. A theology thus can only be really understood when seen in its histori-cal context, in the frame of the influences which produced it.

Let us look then at the background of this movement. The American theological scene of the early twentieth cen-tury was characterized by intense activity—activity which gave to the new evangelical theology its distinctive character.

THE THREAT TO ORTHODOXY

At the beginning of the twentieth century, orthodox the-ology was being challenged from several sources. Some of these threats were external to the church; some were inter-nal. The account of two different reactions to these threats, and the conflict between these two responses, constitutes the story of the modernist-fundamentalist controversy.[1]

One of the areas of major friction was natural science. To be sure, such conflict was not without precedent. One of the church's first great struggles with science had been fought in the sixteenth and seventeenth centuries over the Copernican system of astronomy. Believing that the Bible taught that the earth was the center of the solar system, and strongly influenced by Aristotelianism, many theologians resisted the Copernican view. When it became quite firmly established, however, the church found it necessary to re-consider its view, and concluded that its interpretation of certain Biblical passages had simply been faulty. While such an adjustment was not made without some painful effort, Christian theology found with passing years that it could live with the Copernican astronomy.

More intense, however, were the twentieth-century disputes, both in the number of points of difficulty and in the cruciality of the issues involved. This was particularly dramatized in the evolution debate. Most theologians had interpreted the creation account in Genesis as teaching that man had been made by a unique act of creation. Without employing any pre-existing form of life, God had simply taken dust from the earth, formed it into the body of man, breathed into it the breath of life, and a living human being had resulted. Many had assumed also that Genesis 1 taught that all the species of animal life had been originated by a series of acts of instantaneous creation, distributed over a period of six twenty-four-hour days. Biology now presented an alternative view.

In *the Origin of Species,* published in 1859, Charles Darwin argued that all forms of life had come into existence by a process called evolution. Beginning with the simplest forms of life, progressively more complex forms had developed. Certain changes, called mutations, had arisen in given species. Individuals possessing some of these variations were better able to adapt to their environment than those without them. In the competition for food and life, the former survived, and their offspring were born with these desirable variations. Over a long period of time this process moved onward, and ultimately produced man. While Darwin did not deny the existence of God, he felt that the divine being was no longer required as an explanatory concept. Certainly the acts of special creation were now superfluous.

Geology was another field of emerging conflict with the orthodox tradition. The Irish Archbishop James Ussher had calculated on the basis of the chronological data of the Old Testament that creation had taken place (presumably within a week) about 4,004 years before Christ's birth. This had been accepted by most Christians as being the approximate age of the earth. Geology, however, was now developing means of determining the age of the earth and was arriving at an estimate several times Ussher's figure. As these methods of dating grew increasingly precise, the problem became accentuated.

Still another area of tension was anthropology. The orthodox theology, following again the Ussher chronology, had held that man had been on the earth approximately 6,000 years. All human beings were believed to have descended from a single primal pair, Adam and Eve. Certain significant doctrines, such as that of men by nature beginning their lives with a spiritual taint or corruption, seemed to rest upon this latter conception.

Anthropologists were finding what appeared to be human forms which had to be dated much earlier than 4004 B.C. The indications of culture found in connection with these early specimens were such that it seemed as if the term "human" must be applied to them. In addition, there was evidence which rendered suspect the view that all men had come from a common origin.

It was not only natural science, however, that was proving troublesome to the orthodox theology. Philosophy

seemed to threaten the structure that had been erected.
During the middle ages, philosophy had been regarded as
the handmaiden of theology, providing rational proofs of
the existence of theology's major object, God. As time went
by, this synthesis of theology and philosophy began to
dissolve.

Particularly instrumental in this breakdown was David
Hume. Hume was an empiricist, that is, one who believes
that knowledge comes through man's five senses. Hume
argued that by this means of knowledge, one cannot prove
the Christian God, as Thomas Aquinas and other theologians had maintained. There were several reasons for this.
One was that an infinite cause (God) cannot be inferred
from a finite effect (the world). If this world must have
been caused (as the "cosmological" argument maintained),
only a cause sufficiently great to produce this limited world
is required. How does one prove that this is the God of
Christianity? Hume even challenged the idea of cause.
From an analysis of experience we cannot deduce the idea
of cause as a necessary connection between two events. All
we can find is a constant conjunction. Because A is always
followed by B, we come to think of A as the cause of B.
How many times, however, have we seen a world being
created by a God? Arguments such as these seriously shook
the belief that the existence of God could be proven philo-
sophically. Yet even more severe blows were to come to
orthodox theology.

Immanuel Kant followed the direction set by Hume, but
with some variations. Kant also was concerned with how we
gain knowledge. He was convinced that there are two ele-

ments to knowledge: the mind gives the form (the order or structure) to knowledge, but the content must be supplied by sense experience. The claim of theoretical knowledge of God is empty, since we certainly do not have sense experience of Him. God is brought into Kant's philosophy, but only as a demand of the practical reason: He is needed as a guarantor of our ethical values, of immortality and the like.

The number of persons who believed that metaphysical knowledge was possible was greatly reduced by the arguments of men such as Hume and Kant. Metaphysics is the attempt to give some explanation of the overall nature of reality. Among those who still engaged in this type of activity were some whose views competed with the Christian view, one of the most vital of which was idealism.

Basically, idealism teaches that what is ultimately real about the universe is something more like mind or idea than it is like matter. Thus, all of reality is rational. This sometimes takes the form that all of reality is one great mind thinking, as in the thought of Hegel, or that there is one great person (God) and many smaller persons (men), as in the thought of Lotze. Such views offered an explanation of the nature of things that appealed to some who might otherwise have come to accept the Christian view of God and the world.

Biblical studies also presented difficulty. Since about the time of the Renaissance a method known as historical criticism had been developing. This was an effort to get at what had actually occurred in a given situation. Combined with this was literary criticism, the study of the style and authorship of literary documents. These methods made it possible to determine with some accuracy the age, authorship, and authenticity of certain documents. Such techniques had been employed on secular writings for some time. Now some Biblical scholars suggested that they might be of value in the study of the Christian Scriptures, and proceeded to employ them. The results were not easily harmonized with the traditional view of the Bible.

One conclusion was that a number of the Old Testament books had not been written by the men to whom they were traditionally attributed, and that they may indeed have been the composition of a number of different authors. It appeared also that they might have been composed or at least compiled at a considerably later date than formerly supposed, and that consequently their historical reliability was in question. What seemed to be inaccuracies and factual contradictions were also discovered.

In the face of these problems there were many theologians, pastors, and laymen who felt that the Christian faith, if to be held at all, could not be maintained in its traditional form. For the most part, these men regarded the new learning as dependable. They held that the intellectually respectable and spiritually satisfying position was to accommodate Christian doctrine to the conclusions of science, philosophy, and criticism. Such persons came to be known as liberals or modernists.

Many traditional doctrines were considerably modified. Miracles were regarded as rather unlikely or even impossible. Man was held to be basically good, God was a benevolent Father, and all men were regarded as brothers. The

Bible, seeming to contain numerous errors, could no longer
be treated as in its entirety given to man by God. The idea
that Jesus Christ was a divine being, who by His death on
the cross paid a penalty for the sins of men, was considerably modified. Rather, the death of Christ was seen as having its value in the example which Jesus there gave us of
perfect devotion to the Father.

THE FUNDAMENTALIST REACTION

There were numerous other Christians, however, who
felt that they could not adopt the modernist solution to the
problem.[2] To them the modernist had given up an essential
part of Christianity. They must preserve these doctrines,
rejecting if necessary the modern learning that was threat-
ening them. These were the conservatives. Among the doctrinal essentials to which they held were the following: the
substitutionary theory of the atonement (the view that
Jesus Christ had died in the place of sinful men, paying the
penalty for man's sin); the virgin birth and bodily resurrection of Jesus; the belief that the Holy Spirit had so influenced the writers of the Bible that their writings were not
merely their words, but the very words of God, and thus
completely free from error.

These conservatives felt that the issue was grave: the
preservation of Christianity. Such a concern transcended
denominational lines, and consequently several transde-
nominational efforts resulted from their common convictions.

The initial form of fellowship was the Bible conference.
Here conservative pastors and laymen came together for

several days of Bible messages. Frequently these were largely devoted to the doctrine of the future return of Jesus Christ and related subjects. Beginning in 1876, these conferences had a profound influence upon conservative Protestantism.

Probably the best-known and most significant of the conferences was the Niagara Bible Conference. As these theologians and pastors worshiped and studied together, they sought to defend the Christian faith as they understood it, and to oppose the threats to orthodoxy. In 1895 the Niagara group put forth what may have been the first list of fundamentals. They insisted that there were certain indispensable and irreducible doctrines which the Christian church must maintain. These were the inerrancy of the Scriptures, the deity of Christ, His virgin birth, His substitutionary atonement, His physical resurrection, and His coming bodily return to earth.

In 1909 there was a development which helped to define and identify the conservative element. Feeling the need for an articulate statement of the basic orthodox doctrines and of a polemic against the rising liberalism, two wealthy California laymen, Lyman and Milton Stewart, invested heavily in the defense of the traditional view of Christianity. They financed the publication and distribution of a series of articles called *The Fundamentals*.

Most of the writers were well-trained, careful scholars. Included in the list were men of such stature as James Orr, Benjamin B. Warfield, John C. Ryle, H. C. G. Moule, M. G. Kyle, Charles Erdman, and others. They represented a certain variety of viewpoints within conservative Protestantism. On such doctrines as the nature of inspiration of the Bible and the relation of Christ's coming to the millennium, no monolithic uniformity characterized their writings. The work done was scholarly, both in content and tone.

These articles were widely circulated. By the time the last volume was published, the Stewart brothers could announce that a total of over three million copies had been published. As a result, those who held to the "fundamentals," usually a list very similar or identical to that declared by the 1895 Niagara Conference, came to be known as "Fundamentalist," a term probably coined by Curtis Lee Laws, the editor of the Baptist periodical, *The Watchman Examiner*. This name formed a convenient title which caught on rather quickly.

Note the nature of fundamentalism's defense at this point: scholarly argument. These men gave a reasoned defense of the conservative position, as well as a cogent refutation of the opposition arguments. In addition to these articles, scholarly conservatives such as Machen and Warfield were, through other channels, persuasively contending for the conservative interpretation of historic Christianity.

As the conservative cause continued to struggle for its life, however, there were certain changes in both its strategy and its tactics. The theory of evolution was being elaborated and refined by men of science, many of whom were not of Christian persuasion. The most effective counter to this was largely absent. If scholarly scientists had been available to evaluate the arguments carefully and competently, accepting those elements which were valid, refuting those which were false, and challenging the uncertain or unclear factors, fundamentalism might have won its battle. But unfortunately such persons became increasingly rare in the movement. The opponents of evolution found it more and more difficult to cope with it on a technically competent level. The result was that the struggle was carried on in two ways.

One was a polemic which did not always do credit to the cause. Sometimes in a spirit of ridicule, sometimes in attacks upon personalities, sometimes in sincere but misguided argument, the fundamentalist sought to maintain his case. One particularly striking instance of this occurred in the *Bible Champion* where an editor told of an experiment which he had performed. He had been to a zoo and had observed that the monkeys, restrained in cages, were not capable of communicating with one another. On the other hand, the humans engaged in conversation and roamed the grounds freely. The monkeys acted precisely like those which he had observed when he was a boy: several whole generations of the creatures had passed and there had been no real progress! He therefore concluded that he had that day seen no evidence for evolution and much evidence for fixity of species.[3]

William Jennings Bryan, the "silver-tongued orator," had become a champion of fundamentalism, sometimes employing arguments of limited sophistication. He noted the argument for evolution on the basis of similarities. There is milk in a coconut, in a milkweed, and in a cow; yet, he said, nobody suggests that they are akin, or that one has evolved from the other.[4]

Legal opposition was the other method employed. In

Tennessee and a number of other states, laws were enacted which made it illegal to teach organic evolution in state-supported schools. In at least one instance the constitutionality of the law was challenged in a test case; this was the famous Scopes trial.

John Scopes, a high-school biology teacher in the small mining town of Dayton, Tennessee, had been arrested and charged with teaching evolution. When he was brought to trial, men of considerable reputation participated in the case. Clarence Darrow, a brilliant lawyer and an agnostic, volunteered his services as defense attorney. He saw the issue as being the constitutionality of the law, which he felt prohibited free inquiry and free teaching. In his judgment the law was based upon ignorance and obscurantism, and he intended to expose it as such.

The forces of the prosecution included Bryan, who also saw a larger principle as being involved in the struggle. He contended that the teaching of evolution was destructive to the morals and subversive to the faith of the sons and daughters of those whose taxes were paying the salaries of the school teachers.

The first part of the trial was comparatively simple and quick: Scopes was found guilty of having broken the law. The latter part, however, produced more controversy and interest. Darrow sought to show what evolution was, and that it was not incompatible with the Biblical account of creation. He called on famous scientists to testify. When Bryan objected strenuously to his procedure, Darrow called him to the stand and inquired about his own views of evolution and Christianity. By this time, news reporters from all over the country were present and the trial was a nation-wide news item. The entire town had taken on a carnival atmosphere.

Darrow believed that Bryan's position was based upon ignorance, and that he sought to expose. He managed to make Bryan reveal that he did not really know what would have happened if the earth had stood still, as Joshua seemed to teach. (Bryan hadn't inquired as to this.) Further, Bryan confessed ignorance as to the civilizations of peoples of the earth other than Christians. He did not know how many languages there were in the world, or the age of the earth, or the exact date of the flood. Bryan appeared as a man who really did not have a sufficiently broad education to argue evolution, and who had not really thought through the implications of his position.

The difficulty is rather clear: the fundamentalist simply was not arguing adequately. As a result, his position was rejected or at least ignored by men of scholarly acumen in various disciplines simply because it did not seem to be consistent with intellectual integrity.

This is not to say that all fundamentalists were of the same type. Some recognized their limitations and did not speak in areas or to issues where they were not qualified. J. Gresham Machen, who, although he avoided the title "fundamentalist," certainly held the cardinal doctrines of the movement, refused to participate in a debate over evolution. This was not because he did not have convictions on the matter, but because as a New Testament specialist he did not feel he had the academic preparation to deal with the subject. There were some genuine scientists in the movement, but unfortunately they were not the ones who made their voices heard and thus projected the public image of fundamentalism.

The predominantly negative attitude was also directed toward theological liberalism. Liberalism had strongly emphasized the "social gospel." It stressed the importance of rectifying the ills in society which tend to produce individual sin. Against this, fundamentalism protested, insisting on the necessity of individual conversion and new birth. The proper order, said the fundamentalist, is first individual righteousness, then social justice.

In giving this Biblically-based priority to the evangelistic enterprise, the fundamentalist overreacted. In his zeal to avoid the liberal's social gospel, he tended to neglect the Biblical dimension of the social application of the gospel, though Jesus Himself had told the parable of the Good Samaritan (Luke 10:30-37) and had indicated that at the last judgment the deeds of kindness done to others would be a major criterion in evaluating the spiritual standing of men (Matthew 25:31-46). Thus the fundamentalist stressed increasingly the salvation of the soul, and bypassed the care of the material needs of man. To the observer, the fundamentalist appeared to be somewhat callous.

A further consequence followed. Because they were particularly under attack and debate, the fundamentals were emphasized. The other great doctrines received scanty treatment. The organic character of revealed truth was neglected, and the relationship of underlying theological principles was not comprehended.

There was also a noticeable shift in attitude. Because

fundamentalism found itself under attack, it developed a defensive mentality. A harsh and uncharitable spirit came to predominate. While again this was not true of all fundamentalists, it was this tendency which came to be associated with the term *fundamentalism*. Within its own ranks, internal suspicion and bickering over minor points of doctrine increased.

The transformation was gradual. From a movement of genuine scholarship, positive statement, and a certain latitude of evangelical position, fundamentalism came to be increasingly a negative, defensive, and reactionary movement with a narrowing of its theological options and an evaporation of scholarship and literary productivity.

Corresponding to it was a diminishing influence of fundamentalism. It came to have little effect upon society, and to be rather little considered as a live option, particularly because of its own withdrawal. Within the denominations also, its power waned. This can be seen clearly by studying the history of a group such as the Presbyterian Church, U.S.A. in the nineteen twenties. At the beginning of the decade the fundamentalists had sufficient strength to capture and maintain positions of leadership. Each year, however, the balance of power ebbed away, so that by the second half of the period it was the liberals who occupied offices of power. This was dramatically manifested when in 1929 Machen and others felt compelled to withdraw from the faculty of Princeton Theological Seminary and found a new school, Westminster, in Philadelphia. They also organized their own board of foreign missions, and, when expelled from the denomination, found it necessary to form a new church, the Orthodox Presbyterian Church. Whereas in the eighteen nineties it was the liberal who was being unseated, it was the fundamentalist who was now being forced to withdraw.

THE RISE OF THE NEW EVANGELICALISM

In view of these factors, it is not surprising that fundamentalism's official influence in the intellectual and ecclesiastical spheres declined. Although some thought that conservative Protestantism would die away, there were, even in the nineteen thirties, several indications of a continuing vitality in the movement.[5]

Fundamentalism was proving successful in evangelism, particularly among the lower and lower-middle classes. Contribution figures also showed the conservatives in a favorable light. The conservative churches seemed to be more productive of leadership than the liberals. Even among men who studied at liberal seminaries and became liberal pastors and theologians, a large number were the products of fundamentalism.

Another area of fundamentalist activity was in foreign missions. For all of the liberal's concern for alleviating social needs, it was the fundamentalist, not the liberal, who, on the foreign mission field, led the way not only in direct evangelism, but in medical work, literature, and education.

Nor was fundamentalism totally devoid of centers of scholarly activity. Schools like Westminster Seminary and Dallas Seminary, founded in the late nineteen twenties, were carrying on the tradition of thorough and dependable scholarship, although they were not engaged in much dialogue with liberalism.

There was still another sign of persisting energy within fundamentalism. Here and there, voices were being raised indicating not only an unhappiness with fundamentalism's plight, but also a dissatisfaction with its methods. It was not until after World War II that those voices were to become louder, more numerous, and more influential. With this was to come also a new development in the history of American Christianity.

An outburst of literary production occurred in the years 1946-48. Some was critical of aspects of fundamentalism and called for a conservative reconstruction. Some was scholarly defense of the conservative theology. In each case, however, it appeared that an evangelical rebirth of letters had begun. Among the works were Carl Henry's *Remaking the Modern Mind* and *The Uneasy Conscience of Modern Fundamentalism,* as well as his series of articles on "The New Evangelicalism" in *Christian Life and Times.* This periodical also carried Ockenga's article "Can Fundamentalism Win America?" in which he answered the question essentially by saying, ". . . not as presently constituted." [6]

Such writings and various institutional developments indicated gradually that a new theology was on the scene. These men felt that later fundamentalism had deviated in several important points from the fundamentalism of 1909, and of the *Fundamentals,* and were calling for a return to the earlier form.

What were the characteristics of the "new evangelicalism"? First, an evangelical social ethic was called for. His-

torically, Protestant orthodoxy had not been satisfied simply
with a statement regarding the gospel and the necessity of
personal faith and decision for individual salvation. It had
insisted that the Christian gospel also has something to say
about social problems, and ought to be applied to these
needs in society.

In the twentieth century, however, this dimension of the
gospel appeared to these men to have been neglected. As
liberalism increasingly identified itself with the great social
reform movements, evangelical Christianity or fundamentalism had reacted and drawn away. It had become negative, being aloof from societal needs and critical of those
who were striving to do something about them. As Ockenga
saw it, the church had too often been on the wrong side of
social problems.

In part, this neglect could also be traced to certain aspects of the doctrinal system of fundamentalism. With a
belief in the total corruption of sinful man's nature and a
conception that the end of the world was coming soon,
many conservatives had drawn the incorrect conclusion
that the only hope was to try to rescue individual sinners
from sin, and not to waste time trying to combat social
ills.

It was not an abandonment of the fundamentalist message that was being called for, however. All of the fundamentals could be unreservedly subscribed to by the new
evangelicals. Rather, they felt that a certain aspect or theme
within evangelicalism had been neglected and needed to be
stressed again. They saw themselves as in no sense a departure from classical orthodoxy, but rather a reinstitution

of it. They were not advocating a social gospel; personal regeneration was still a necessity for individual salvation. A social application of the evangelical gospel was their concern.

A second major theme in this new developing movement within evangelicalism was *apologetics*, defense of the faith. It appeared to these theologians that the conservative forces had definitely lost the battle in the fundamentalist-modernist controversy. It had happened in large part simply because their case had not been persuasively presented. Although the fundamentalist position most closely approximated the truth in religious and spiritual matters, its defense had not been as competent as was desirable.

These men resolved to take up the presentation of the evangelical gospel using the finest of arguments and the most winsome of considerations. They were determined, first, that they would obtain adequate academic preparation in their respective fields, so that the discussion could be carried on with full awareness of the current issues. Further, they would not speak in areas where they were not prepared. The effort of William Jennings Bryan and others to debate biological evolution, a field in which they were scarcely experts, seemed to the new evangelicals to be a serious mistake.

Consequently, the philosophical implications of Biblical theism were to be spelled out. Liberalism had gone in heavily for the philosophy of religion, to the relative neglect of theology, and the form of the Biblical conception of God and His relation to the world had been recast. Philosophical competitors had arisen, and as American evangelicalism failed to state effectively its position, it had been losing its young people. Henry felt that the time had come to bring the philosophers to terms with the Biblical message, rather than vice versa.

The effort followed two major lines. One was to challenge the optimistic mood and philosophic presuppositions of secular and liberal thought. This was the positive presentation of the Christian view, which is quite clearly seen in *Introduction to Christian Apologetics*. Nor were the factual dimensions of Christianity neglected. Bernard Ramm sought to show the historical reliability and the supernatural origin of the Bible.[7]

The relationship of the Christian theology and natural science had been a source of great friction and difficulty in the early part of the century and particularly in the twenties. This problem occupied much of the attention of the new evangelicals. Because they were primarily theologians and philosophers rather than scientists, much of their work concentrated upon the philosophy of science and the methodology and general relationship of the disciplines of science and theology. Such early works as Henry's *Remaking the Modern Mind* and Carnell's *Apologetics* manifested this. Bernard Ramm, though not a scientist, had studied science considerably and read extensively. He came to grips with some of the more specific problems in his book *The Christian View of Science and Scripture*.

A development fitting within this general stream was the organization of the American Scientific Affiliation, which began with the meeting of five Christian scientists in Chicago in September, 1941. With a concern to preserve the faith of young people from the eroding effects of scientific materialism, the Affiliation grew in numbers and in activity and influence. One of the declared purposes of the group was "to prepare literature correlating science and the Holy Scriptures." Men trained in the several special sciences were able to carry on the work in areas where the theologians were not prepared to go.

A third factor of the new movement was evangelism. A movement which possesses scholarly acumen may be able to capture the attention and loyalty of scholars and eventually filter down to the rank and file; but in order to have a rapid and extensive growth and acceptance, a new system of thought must have a popularizer capable of putting the ideas in popular form and of capturing the imagination of the laity. One of the reasons for the rather rapid return of evangelicalism to a position of prominence in American religious life has been the work of Billy Graham.[8]

Graham had grown up in Southern Baptist fundamentalism. He had trained at Bob Jones University, Florida Bible Institute, and Wheaton College. After a pastorate in Western Springs, a suburb of Chicago, he entered full-time evangelistic work with the Youth for Christ organization. About the year 1949 he began to attract attention through his marked success in several evangelistic campaigns— success both in terms of the attendance and the number of persons making "decisions for Christ." Graham's fame spread rapidly, and he was soon conducting mass-scale evangelistic campaigns in cities around the world.

As indicated above, Graham's background was strict fundamentalism. At one time he had even been part-time president of Northwestern Schools in Minneapolis, an institution founded by W. B. Riley, one of the primary leaders in the fundamentalist movement. As Graham's evangelistic ministry developed, however, he came to represent a broadened position. There are several points at which Graham could be said to have strong affinity with the new evangelicalism as thus far described. While he is not in the strict sense of the word a theologian, his influence on conservative Protestantism qualifies him for inclusion in this movement.

First, there has been something of a shift in Graham's thinking toward a less exclusively literal interpretation of Scripture. In his early preaching, Graham gave evidence of a belief in a hell which burned with a physical, not a figurative, fire. Heaven was pictured as a cube, sixteen hundred miles on a side. Later he came to believe that hell's fire may be the burning thirst for God of those who have been eternally banished from His presence. Hell is no less real, however, whether the Bible's words describing it are taken literally or figuratively. Heaven has come to be thought of as a place "beyond our understanding."

A second characteristic of Graham's ministry has been an increasing emphasis on the social implications of the gospel. This can be noticed by anyone who has followed the "Hour of Decision" broadcasts over the years. Graham says that the gospel has both a vertical and a horizontal dimension, and that a gospel preaching only one of these is at best a truncated gospel. He has attempted to maintain a balance of the two factors. He devotes at least a third of his preaching to encouraging and teaching people to apply the principles of Christianity in their personal and social lives. The message of Christianity must be for the whole man. When Graham speaks out on such issues as race relations, he insists that they be considered within the context of man's spiritual depravity and the need for individual regeneration.

Finally, Billy Graham's evangelistic work is "cooperative evangelism." He has shown a desire to work with ministers of varying theological stripe, whether liberal or conservative. In his city-wide campaigns, he prefers that the invitation and planning be done by a group representing the various positions of the theological spectrum.

The name of Billy Graham has become a household word in America and elsewhere. In the past twenty years he has preached to millions of persons. Several of his major campaigns have been telecast on national networks, and he has a regularly scheduled radio program. *Decision* magazine, prepared by his organization, is sent into millions of homes. He has been interviewed countless times on television programs and in leading magazines, all of it helping to lend impetus to the growing evangelical rebirth.

Another dominant note in the new evangelicalism is the emphasis on education. As more and more Christian colleges and theological seminaries moved into liberalism, fundamentalism increasingly drew its pastoral leadership from three-year Bible institutes. With the close of the war and the large numbers of veterans attending college, the educational level of the general populace began to rise, and rapidly. The new evangelicals saw a need for quality education of evangelical leaders to meet the challenge.

One result of this concern was the founding of Fuller Theological Seminary. For many years, Rev. Charles E. Fuller had carried on a ministry as an evangelist and Bible teacher, and had founded and directed the "Old-Fashioned

Revival Hour" radio broadcast. He had also entertained hopes of establishing an evangelical interdenominational seminary on the West Coast. On Sunday afternoon, June 15, 1947, Fuller announced on his radio program that the Fuller Seminary would open on October 1, at Pasadena, California.

The objective of the planners of the school was stated clearly: to establish a school unexcelled in academic prowess, yet based firmly upon the conservative interpretation of Christianity. The founders intended to accomplish their aim by bringing together a collection of evangelical scholars such as had not worked together since the days of Machen, Wilson, Hodge, and others at old Princeton Seminary.

The faculty, while initially small in number, listed illustrious names. Harold Ockenga was the president, the plans being for him to serve *in absentia* for the first two years. Dr. Wilbur Smith of Moody Bible Institute, an author, editor, and bibliophile, was to teach English Bible and apologetics. As professor of New Testament and Greek, Everett Harrison of Dallas Theological Seminary was appointed. From the faculty of Northern Baptist Theological Seminary came Harold Lindsell as registrar and acting professor of missions, and Carl Henry as professor of systematic theology and philosophy of religion, and acting dean. Each of these men was an experienced seminary professor.

The beginning was a small one, with just four full-time professors and forty students. The school continued to grow, however, so that by 1958 the faculty numbered fifteen fulltime men, all but one of whom possessed at least one earned doctorate.

Fuller Seminary was not the only sign of educational emphasis. Other seminaries raised the standards of their educational programs. Several evangelical Christian colleges obtained regional accreditation. The National Association of Evangelicals appointed a Commission on Education to foster cooperation and interchange among conservative Christian educational institutions and to upgrade Christian education at all levels.

The theologians were concerned to prepare themselves thoroughly, and sought at least a part of their preparation outside the evangelical sphere. We find them attending leading secular graduate schools and liberal seminaries for their graduate study, to help preserve them from both the suspicion and the fact of narrowness of outlook.

Still a further development was the establishment of the Evangelical Theological Society. This began as a result of a proposal by faculty members of the Gordon Divinity School for a permanent organization of conservative Biblical and theological scholars to foster theological scholarship. On December 27 and 28, 1949, some sixty theologians of various denominations met in Cincinnati, Ohio, drafted a constitution, and brought into being the Evangelical Theological Society. The group has continued to meet annually to hear and discuss papers on scholarly topics, and, at the fifteenth anniversary meeting in December, 1964, numbered 447 full members, plus 151 associate members and 109 student associates. While by no means all of the members of the society could be classified as "new evangelicals," the general aims and activities of the group are indicative of the rebirth of evangelical scholarship typifying the new evangelicalism.

There also were conspicuous developments in publication. As already indicated, these men believed in making public their scholarship and thought, and the result was a flow of articles and books from their pens. The theological world in general was made aware of a new literary life in the conservative camp.

In 1956 the new evangelicalism projected an official organ, a fortnightly periodical named *Christianity Today*. Carl Henry was called from his teaching post at Fuller Seminary to serve as editor. In the beginning, the magazine was sent free of charge to theological students and clergymen of various theological persuasions, assuring it of a wide circulation.

The purpose of the new magazine was stated by the editor in the first issue.[9] The magazine, he said, aimed to express historical Christianity to the present generation. It was the conviction of the founders that theological liberals had failed to meet the moral and spiritual needs of the people. The editors accepted unreservedly the "complete reliability of the written Word of God." It was also the conviction of the editors that the Scriptures teach the doctrine of plenary inspiration of the Bible. Because this doctrine had often been misrepresented and misunderstood, it was to be one of the aims of the magazine to state the Biblical concept of inspiration. Other doctrines to be presented and defended were those of God, Christ, man, salvation, and the last things.

This statement of intent also shows a concern for the social aspect of the gospel, it being the aim to present the implications of the total gospel message for every area of life, something fundamentalism had sometimes failed to do. Further, *Christianity Today* recognized that modern scientific theory had often had a dissolving effect upon religion. The magazine thus aimed to set forth the unity of the divine revelation in nature and in Scripture. *Christianity Today* dedicated itself "to the presentation of the reasonableness and effectiveness of the Christian gospel." This it undertook to do with sincere Christian love for those who might differ with them, or with whom they might have to differ.

Another feature of the new evangelicalism was an emphasis upon and effort toward unity.[10] Its spokesmen felt one of the great tragedies of conservative Protestantism was its fragmentizing tendency. Although most evangelicals had more in common than they had dividing them, they were going their separate ways, duplicating efforts. Sometimes minor doctrinal points, such as the minutiae of the doctrine of last things, seemed to be keeping these segments apart.

To the new evangelicals this was a deplorable situation. The potential strength of evangelicalism was being dissipated by the splintering of the movement. These thinkers consequently called for a Biblically-based ecumenism, or cooperative effort. Already in existence was an organization known as the Federal Council of Churches of Christ (later, the National Council of Churches of Christ), largely based upon liberal doctrine and philosophy of action. The moderate conservatives did not feel that they could participate in and cooperate with this group. A group on the extreme right edge of Protestantism organized itself in 1940 into the American Council of Churches; it was a group quite reactionary in spirit and much devoted to polemic against the National Council. No one who belonged to the National Council could be a part of the American Council. This attitude, however, was also repugnant to a number of conservatives. Several moderate conservatives after mutual consultation issued a joint letter to a large number of Christian leaders, calling for a meeting on April 7-9, 1942, in St. Louis. From this emerged an organization known as the National Association of Evangelicals. The group was to be positive in character, stressing the doctrines held in common, and particularly the deity and Lordship of Jesus Christ, and the inspiration and consequent infallibility of the Scriptures. It sought to lead evangelicals into fellowship and cooperative effort in such areas as evangelism, education, publication, radio broadcasting, missions, and social action. Although these persons had definite objections to the ideology and practices of the National Council, they did not intend to engage in any substantial criticism of that group. Membership in the National Council of Churches would not bar an individual church or denomination from inclusion in the National Association of Evangelicals, provided of course that he could conscientiously subscribe to the principles of the latter group.

The basis for cooperation was to be spiritual unity: all believers in Christ are one in fellowship. It was a cooperative fellowship of individuals and groups, rather than in any sense a "superchurch."

The organization of the NAE antedated the visible arising of the group which we are here terming "the new evangelicals." As they began to make their voices heard, however, there was a determined and continued call for unity among evangelicals, and this was particularly an approval of the NAE. Harold Ockenga was the first NAE president and gave the keynote address at the first full convention.

Through the work of the NAE and its several commissions and subsidiary agencies, cooperation among evangelicals has been effected in a number of areas. The Evangelical Theological Society, already mentioned, was one parallel development on the scholarly level.

A system of thought is not simply a set of ideas, held abstractly from life and persons. The theological conceptions of this movement are inseparably bound up with the personalities and lives of the men involved in it. Upon examination of the lives of these men one discerns a noticeable similarity of pattern. Typically, they came from a conservative or even fundamentalist background. While their undergraduate training was generally in a conservative school, they then sought graduate experience at a leading liberal or secular institution. Somewhere in this development the men became aware of the shortcomings of fundamentalism, and the need for a reconstruction.

An excellent example is Edward John Carnell. Born in 1919, Carnell was the son of a Northern Baptist pastor. He attended Wheaton College, where he majored in philosophy under Gordon Haddon Clark, graduating in 1941. He then took his theological training at Westminster Theological Seminary, receiving his Th.B. and Th.M. degrees in 1944. Majoring in apologetics with Cornelius Van Til, he was awarded the apologetics prize. After a brief pastorate at Marblehead, Massachusetts, he matriculated at Harvard

University Divinity School. Majoring in systematic theology, he received the S.T.M. degree in 1946 and the Th.D. in 1948, his doctoral dissertation dealing with the theology of Reinhold Niebuhr. During this time he assumed teaching duties at Gordon College and Divinity School in Boston and in 1948 joined the faculty of the new Fuller Seminary. Having also studied philosophy at Boston University under the direction of Edgar Sheffield Brightman, he was in 1949 awarded the Ph.D. degree by that institution. In addition to all this, he had in 1948 written an apologetics textbook which won the $5,000 first prize in the Wm. B. Eerdmans Publishing Co. evangelical textbook contest. Young Carnell had accomplished a great deal in his thirty years.

He tells of how he came to realize the need of a vigorous output of evangelical theological literature. As a graduate student at Harvard, he observed that conservative theology was not even seriously considered; it simply was ignored. He concluded that what was needed was a surge of evangelical scholarship and literary production, and resolved that he would be a part of it. This same course was followed by others of the "new evangelical" persuasion as well.

SUMMARY

At the beginning of the twentieth century, orthodox theology was under attack. Developments in natural science, philosophy, and Biblical studies were undermining several of the cardinal doctrines of orthodoxy. In the face of this, certain Christians (termed liberals, or modernists) abandoned or modified some of the doctrines.

Other Christians, however, felt that certain irreducible minimums of the Christian faith must be retained. They sought to defend these teachings against the threats to them. They came to be known as fundamentalists. Gradually, however, they lost the battle in the major denominations and in the culture in general. They were forced to withdraw or become minority groups.

There seem to be reasons for this loss. Adequate answers were not being given to the intellectual problems. Evolution, for example, was being debated by fundamentalists without proper scientific training. Fundamentalism also was neglecting the social aspect, or social application, of its gospel message. Its position became narrowed in the twenties from its earlier form; it developed a defensive mentality, and it cut itself off from culture.

Following World War II, a new development took place in conservative Christianity. A group of well-trained young scholars arose, determined to state the evangelical position competently, avoiding the errors into which fundamentalism had fallen. This movement, the new evangelicalism, stressed several themes: social ethics, apologetics, evangelism, education, and unity.

II

The Principle of Authority

John Jones had never won anything in his life. Yet all he had to do to enter the contest was to write his name on the slip of paper and deposit it in a box at the grocery store. He thought nothing more of it until one day his telephone rang. He had won the $10,000 first prize! As unbelievable as it seemed, it was true, and soon a certified check was in his hands.

That was not the last time John's phone was to ring in the next few weeks. When the local newspaper announced his good fortune, John's friends offered their congratulations. Many of them had good advice. "I know of a place where you can really make your money grow," said one man. "A friend of mine has just founded a new manufacturing company and he needs capital. You could become a partner with that $10,000." Other friends had hot tips, too. One knew of a stock which was about to split. Banks, stockbrokers, salesmen—all kept John's line hot.

"I'm so confused with all this advice, I don't know what to do with my money," John complained. "Life was simple before this happened."

Mr. Jones' problem was one of authority. He wanted to invest his money in the best way, but whose advice was he to follow? Who really was qualified to direct him? Who was an authority?

The same problem occurs in the realm of religion. If one asks, "What should I believe and why?" or "How should I conduct my life?" He gets many different answers. A glance at the yellow pages of a large city telephone directory reveals a variety of religious groups. The Chicago yellow pages, for example, divide the classification "churches" into 84 subdivisions.

What is one to believe, and why? How do I know which of the many claimed gods is the true one, and thus the one to be believed in? How do I know what God is like and what He expects of me? Is there anything in religion which demands that I think about it in one certain way and not another? Is there some principle, society, person, or document which has the right to prescribe religious belief? [1]

Authority, in general, is the right to command belief or action. It functions in many different areas of life. When a policeman blows his whistle or sounds his siren and says, "Pull over to the curb," he is exercising the authority which society has delegated to him, and he is usually obeyed. A private citizen who steps out into an intersection and tries to flag cars to the curb might end up with the tread marks of someone's snow tires on his body. The policeman has an authority which the private citizen does not.

Authority of a different type is demonstrated when one's medical doctor tells him, "You have an infection. Take these pills and go to bed and rest." Authority may be accepted or rejected, but it is based upon right, power, or knowledge.

In the ultimate analysis, of course, God Himself is the authority in belief and conduct—if there is a God. Certainly an almighty Creator has the right to prescribe what His creatures ought to believe and what they ought to do. This, however, does not really settle the question. The further problem is how God expresses or exercises this authority. A king or emperor cannot, or at least does not, directly exercise his authority over every individual subject of his realm, but entrusts it to numerous officials and organizations, and publishes it in various documents and edicts. Similarly, God has delegated His authority, but the question is really *where* and *how?* What institution or document possesses the right to prescribe just as God Himself does?

THE SELF-MANIFESTATION OF GOD

Man has at all times and in every nation sought to know God. This cannot be doubted, for religions abound. Yet the very fact of these many and contradictory religions is eloquent testimony of man's inability to discover much about God by his own effort. It is difficult to believe that the Hindu and the Christian, or even the liberal and conservative Christian, are speaking about the same god.

It is not surprising that man's intellectual attempts to discover God end in confusion. God and man are very different beings. God is unlimited in His power and knowledge. Just as a dog or a cat cannot discover his master's mind by study or thought, neither can man search out God.

Just as the master must take the initiative in communicating himself to the animal, so must God "reveal." Himself to man. God is known by man because He has made Himself known to man. This He has done in two ways.

The first is *general* revelation. Man stands outside at night, gazes up at the stars in awe, and exclaims, "There is a god." That was the testimony of the psalmist who said, "The heavens declare the glory of God; and the firmament sheweth his handywork" (Psalm 19:1, KJV). Man studies the intricate structure of the human eye, or looks within at his moral nature, and comes to much the same conclusion. This is because God is the One who has made all these things and, like the craftsman, has left His signature or His distinguishing mark upon His product.[2]

All men at all times have access to this general revelation. Nature, with its awesome greatness and impressive regularity, can be observed by anyone with normal sense perception. Any human being can search his heart and discover the inward law written there. This inward law is not necessarily some moral code inscribed upon man's psyche, but it is the impulse that he ought to do right, and the sense that there is some meaningful distinction between right and wrong.

The general revelation is somewhat incomplete, however. By it, man is enabled to know that there is a God, and that He is great and powerful, but little else. (See Romans 1:19, 20). Man really does not, by this, come to the kind of knowledge of God which results in salvation.

The major reason why the general or natural revelation does not accomplish more is sin, which is man's rebellion against God and his failure to do God's will perfectly. Sin is like a great cloud between man and God, obscuring man's vision of his Master. It is like an argument which takes place between two friends. When it arises, it mars the friendship, and makes it impossible for the one really to understand the other, because he can no longer empathize with him.[3]

At this point, one might be inclined to despair, if he is unable to know God. Yet despair in itself may not be a bad thing if it brings him to realize that he needs additional help from God. Here the new evangelicals are intensely optimistic, for they insist that God has given a *special* revelation which goes beyond the general revelation in its clarity, intensity, and detail. It answers for man the all-important question: "What does God require of me, and what must I do to please Him?"

There is a note of confidence and assurance in the voice of the new evangelical when he quotes from the Bible. Without qualification or hesitation, Billy Graham declares, "The Bible says, 'Believe on the Lord Jesus Christ and thou shalt be saved.'" He says this with emphasis and authority, for like other conservatives he believes that these are not merely the words of the Apostle Paul spoken to a Philippian jailer some nineteen hundred years ago; they are actually God's very words to us, true and dependable. For conservatives, "the Bible says" is equivalent to "God says." God has taken special steps to make Himself known to man, and this revelation is now available in the Bible.

How did the Bible come to have this status? The new evangelicals indicate that God has utilized several means to make Himself known, and that revelation is primarily the active process of self-communication. They observe that there is a prominent note of *condescension* on God's part. Because God is so far above men's understanding, God has had to adapt Himself and His message to the level and the understanding of man. Like an adult who both literally and figuratively bends down and whispers in the child's ear, in a child's terminology, so God has given the knowledge of Himself in human or earthly form.[4]

God, in other words, uses forms and means which are normal to human experience. What is new and different, though, is that God takes this human form and uses it to accomplish His purposes, communicating through it. Dreams, for instance, are normal elements in human life. It is not the dream in itself that is supernatural; it is that God, through dreams, speaks to man. We are not confronted with the dream-in-itself, as if dreams had some inherent revelation-bearing powers. Neither are we confronted with revelation-in-itself, as if revelation could come to man's consciousness apart from any medium. It is the combination of human form and divine content that constitutes an effective communication.

There is a certain parallel between God's revelation and the incarnation. Jesus, in coming to the earth, did not merely appear as bare deity. He took upon Himself the form of man, genuine humanity. In itself, there was not necessarily anything unusual or supernatural about the humanity of Jesus. He was probably of a physical stature and an intelligence quotient within the customary range of normal human individuals. Yet there was a uniqueness, for the Second Person of the divine trinity was actually combined with the normal human individual.

This means that when God describes Himself in His revelation, He speaks of Himself not as He is in Himself, but as we conceive of Him. For example, as John Calvin pointed out, when the Bible speaks of God as being angry with men, we ought not really to suppose that He feels toward men this same emotion as men do, but rather we ought to accommodate the mode of speech to our own sense.

God's revelation uses human language. The Hebrew and Greek languages were not some supernatural tongues especially created for the Bible; they were human languages employed by the Holy Spirit for the service of special revelation. The languages also brought along their cultures, those of the Greek and Hebrew. Revelation actually takes place *through* the culture.

Revelation, in addition to being *anthropic,* or in human form, is also *analogical.* While God cannot show us Himself as He really is, if the revelation is to be real knowledge and in any way a map of Himself, it must be analogical. This means that God selects those elements, or factors, from our realm of experience which bear a resemblance to the truth about Himself. While they are not perfect replicas of God, they are nonetheless adequate reproductions. Their relationship to the original is more like that of a sketch or a cartoon than a blueprint or a portrait. There is a certain analogy between some elements of man's knowledge and some portions of God's truth, and God employs the analogy for His purposes.

Objection sometimes is raised on the grounds that we

cannot really know by analogy unless we have some way of knowing that there actually is an analogy. In the equation $x:4 = 1:2$, we can calculate the value of x because we know that it bears the same relationship to 4 as 1 bears to 2. How do we know, however, that God as He is in Himself is proportionate to those elements of our experience through which He reveals Himself? The answer is that we do not have any independent knowledge of it. The revelation itself includes the disclosure that God has chosen expressions and concepts that are analogical.

An example would be the expression "Heavenly Father." We have no way of knowing God apart from His self-disclosure so as to see that He is somehow "like" a human father. We are told, however, "As a father pities his children, so the Lord pities those who fear him" (Psalm 103: 13, RSV).

This, then, is the manner of God's communication: that it is anthropic and analogical. What are the specific means, however, of this revelation? What has gone before has implied that one does not meet God directly or know God's thoughts directly. The knowledge of God is mediated through several *means,* or *modalities.*[5]

The first means by which God has revealed Himself is by His acts. God is a God of history. Unlike the watchmaker-god who supposedly made the world and then left it to run by itself, God has been actively at work within the span of time and within human existence, seeking to accomplish His purpose. These very acts have made known to man something of God's nature.

Thus, we can turn to the great series of events known as

the Exodus. Here were the people of Israel enslaved in Egypt and crying out for relief. God in pity did not simply turn a deaf ear, but sent His servant Moses to be the deliverer. In order to persuade the king of Egypt to let the people go, God sent a series of miraculous plagues. When the Egyptians pursued the Israelites, God performed another astounding miracle in stopping the waters of the Red Sea so that the Israelites might pass over safely, and then letting the waters roll back again in order to destroy the enemy. In this, God demonstrated His mighty power. Time and time again, the children of Israel turned from God, and yet each time He forgave them, showing His faithfulness. Because of their continued stubborn rebellion, God did not let any of the original group (except Joshua and Caleb) enter the promised land. In that manner, He revealed His holiness and justice.

Other great deeds of God also demonstrated His nature. They were, so to speak, God's pantomimes; yet they were not alone. Together with them we also find the second modality, God's *speech*.

The Bible contains the repeated expression, ". . . the word of the Lord came to ——, saying: . . . ." There is a consciousness that God has spoken, and that the prophet is merely communicating what he has received. This speaking may come in one of several forms.

There is the voice of God coming in audible words, which was undoubtedly the case in John 12:28, where there evidently was a voice that could be heard by all, even though it was definitely not recognized or understood by some who were present. Although God may not have the organs of speech (tongue, lips, vocal cords, lungs), it is certainly possible for an Almighty God to create sound miraculously, or to use the speech of an angel.

Further, there is silent or inward hearing of the Word of God. Just as a person may "hear sounds inside his head," or a tune may run through his mind, it may be that the voice of God was "heard" by men in situations where there was no audible sound. This should not be conceived of as some instance of mental abnormality, but rather as a way of God making Himself known.

A final form of the divine speech is "concursive inspiration." As the prophet or apostle spoke or wrote, the Holy Spirit moved along with his action in such a way that the thing written or spoken was also the Word of God. The writer or speaker may not even have been conscious of any special influence of the Holy Spirit. Nonetheless, the product was as genuinely God's speech as if it had been audibly spoken.

The most complete mode of God's revelation is the incarnation. God did not simply stand outside the stream of human experience, reaching in periodically with His actions and His words. For a period of time the Second Person of the trinity, God the Son, actually became man and lived a divine life within the realm of human experience. The testimony of John is that he and others really saw, heard, handled deity. Jesus Christ was God living on earth. The words that He spoke, the love that He showed, the works that He performed were the words, the love, and the deeds of God. Again, it was not a direct and unmediated presence of God, since the deity was combined with humanity, but it was nonetheless a real presence of God.

These then are the means through which God has made

himself known to man. The new evangelicals would insist strenuously that one of the results of special revelation is genuine knowledge of God. Neo-orthodoxy has stressed the idea of revelation being an *encounter* with God, rather than communication of information about God. The new evangelicals, however, would say that these two are not to be separated, but rather must be conjoined. The statement, "What God reveals is God, not information about Himself," is answered by the query, "But how does He reveal Himself?" and the rather forthright reply, "He reveals Himself by communicating the truth about Himself." This becomes the basis for a personal encounter.

THE PRESERVATION OF THE REVELATION

Suppose that God has actually revealed Himself; that He has spoken, acted, and even come—in order that man might know Him. A problem still remains. Would not this value be lost when the act of God was past, when His works were forgotten, or when Jesus Christ no longer walked personally, visibly, and bodily upon the earth? If the revelation was to be authoritative and effective—not merely to the persons to whom it came, but to various people at different times—it would be necessary for it to be preserved.

Preservation of the revelation might have been done in several ways. It might have been by oral tradition: those who experienced the revelation might have passed it on by word of mouth to others, who in turn would have told still others, and so on down the line. Indeed, new evangelicals hold that the revelation was preserved at least for a time by such means. It could also have been kept by normal means of writing: the person to whom God revealed Himself could have sat down and, as accurately as he could, recorded what he remembered of the account. That he would have done simply by the use of his abilities of insight, observation, and recall.

Both means of preservation would have suffered from a major defect, however: there would have been no real guarantee of the accuracy of the record. Anyone who has played a parlor game in which a brief story is whispered to one person, who then whispers it to the next, and so on, knows that oral transmission is subject to corruption. The author once suffered a bruised lip while playing in a high-school football game. By the next afternoon, however, he had "lost three or four teeth," and he suffered more from the passing of the story than from the injury itself. Similarly, a professor who reads in an essay examination an account of what he is supposed to have said (and which the student can document from his notes), knows that speech can be misunderstood, misinterpreted, or confused. An oral account or a fallible human recording cannot really suffice where matters of life and death are involved. Just at the crucial point the record may be in error.

The other alternative, according to the orthodox or conservative theologian, is inspiration. This is a term explaining the writing of Scripture, which means that the writers wrote under a supernatural influence of the Holy Spirit. This rendered their writings (the Bible) an accurate record of the revelation; or to put it differently, what they wrote was actually the Word of God. Hence the value of the revelation is preserved to later generations.

Inspiration is not held by the new evangelicals simply out

of practical concern, however. The Bible makes this claim
for itself. This may seem to be a circular argument: "We
know that the Bible is inspired because it says so. We know
that what the Bible says is true because it is inspired. Therefore, it is true that the Bible is inspired." No circle is involved, however. Rather, the argument is more like a spiral.
When the Bible is cited as saying that it is given by inspiration, it is not being appealed to as an inspired book. It is
simply being allowed to speak for itself, just as a witness in
court. The truth or falsity of its claim must be established
on other grounds.

When one asks about the Christian view of the inspiration and authority of the Bible, his first inquiry ought logically to concern the view held and taught by Jesus Christ.
Since He is the Founder and Definer of this historical religion, His view would seem to be of utmost significance. If
we are to accept His authority on other matters, we logically ought to do so in this area. In seeking to determine
Christ's view of the Scriptures, we are dependent upon the
New Testament itself. Yet we are not appealing to it as
being divinely inspired, but simply as a dependable historical document, which it would appear to be.[6]

First, Christ seemed to accept the view of the Old Testament held by the Jews of His day. As Carnell points out,
there was in the society which Jesus entered a conception of
the sacredness of the Scriptures. He did not in any way deny
or contradict that conception. Whereas He frequently challenged the particular interpretation of Scripture which was
held, or the application which was made of it, He seems
never to have disapproved of the basic view of it as the very

oracle of God, and as therefore binding upon man. Even radical critics would acknowledge that Christ actually held this view of the Scriptures, by which He meant the Old Testament.

This is indicated not only by His own testimony, but also by that of His opponents. There were at the time of Christ two holy things in Israel: the Temple and the Scriptures. Jesus gave up the former, indicating that not one stone would be left upon another, and that the geographical place of worship was not of crucial significance. For this, He was accused by the Jews who examined carefully all that He said. Had He in any sense disagreed with the prevailing view of Scriptures, they would no doubt have risen in protest; yet we read of no complaint against Him on that point. The simplest explanation is merely that He held and expressed basically the same view of the nature of Scripture as they.

It might be supposed that Jesus gave adherence to the Old Testament as a whole or in general, but not as to specific details. This must be challenged, however. Jesus' statements often depended for their force upon a single detail. In Matthew 22:44 (KJV), for instance, He said, "The Lord said unto *my Lord. . . .*" The whole meaning turns on the word *Lord,* or more exactly on the possessive suffix *my* (a single letter in Hebrew). In John 10:34 His statement is meaningless unless the word "gods" (and in the plural number) is authoritative. Jesus seemed also to display a rather strict view of Scripture's authority when He said ". . . the scripture cannot be broken." (John 10:35, KJV).

Nor will it do to say that Jesus simply accommodated

Himself to the prevailing religious opinion. When we examine the Gospels, we find that Jesus challenged any religious conceptions which were false, mistaken, or distorted.
In other areas than the Scriptures He did not hesitate to set
Himself against the tradition, even employing the Old Testament to refute the received religious opinions of scribes
and Pharisees. The apostles held the same view of Scripture
as Jesus, using the Old Testament in such a way as to imply
its authoritativeness. The fact that "it is written" establishes
it as being so.

Just what is the nature of inspiration of the Bible? What
does it involve? How much of the Bible is inspired? Is all of
it, or are only certain parts? Are all parts equally inspired,
or is there variation between one type of literature and
another?

The new evangelicals espouse the view generally referred
to as *plenary* inspiration: that the whole Bible, not just
parts, is the product of the inspiring work of the Holy Spirit.
This again is based upon the Bible's own witness to itself.
Paul's statement to Timothy said, *"All* Scripture is given by
inspiration of God . . ."* (II Timothy 3:16, KJV). The New
Testament writers seemed to regard the entire Old Testament as one unified whole, so that their certification of it as
inspired involved the books of law, prophecy, and poetry.
Further, they seemed to accept the writings of one another
as of the same character as the Old Testament. An example
of this is found in Peter's reference to Paul's writings (II
Peter 3:15, 16). There is still, of course, the problem of the
canon—namely, which books properly deserve to be included in "the Scriptures"—but at least the claim is made

that all Scripture, not merely certain portions, is the result of divine inspiration.[7]

Some views of inspiration, particularly in liberalism, hold that the Bible was inspired, but not equally in all its parts. This distinction is steadfastly opposed by the new evangelicals, who consider that all parts of the Bible are inspired, although not for the same immediate purpose. Some portions are intended to convey or preserve historical data, other parts have a practical or devotional value. While the genealogies may not be as edifying as the Psalms or Paul's Letters, one should not conclude that there is a difference in inspiration. Such a conclusion would assume the liberal's premise, "That is inspired which is inspiring."

The other set of questions deals with the degree of inspiration. How inspired is the Bible, or what did this really involve? Traditionally there have been several theories of inspiration.

The *intuition* theory says that the Biblical writers produced their works, not out of any special stimulation by the Holy Spirit, but simply by exercising certain gifts of religious genius with which they were endowed. Just as there is musical aptitude or artistic aptitude, so, according to this theory, there is religious aptitude. The prophets and apostles were simply men who were gifted to an unusual degree with ability to discover religious truth. They were religious geniuses.

A second view is termed the *illumination* theory, which emphasizes a particular influence of the Holy Spirit upon the Scripture writer at the moment of writing, but maintains that this merely involves a heightening or stimulation of the powers or abilities already possessed. There is no communication of new information. Like a "pep pill," or a "memory pill," the Holy Spirit stimulated the mind of the prophet or apostle so that he was able to discern truth which otherwise would have been unrecognizable to him.

The *dynamic* theory maintains that the Holy Spirit so guided and controlled the person that his thoughts were the thoughts that God would have had him think. In his selection of words to express the thoughts in writing, however, the man had freedom of choice, the only limitation being that the words should faithfully preserve the content of the thought.

In the *verbal* view of inspiration, the work of the Holy Spirit is so intensive that it even results in the choice of one word, rather than another. Thus the words of the Bible are genuinely the words of God.

Finally, it is possible to hold that the Bible was a *dictation*, in which God told the man exactly what to write. It is more common to find theologians accused of holding this view than actually avowing it.

That dictation was not the dominant or normal form of inspiration seems apparent to the new evangelicals from an examination of the Bible. The different writers use differing styles and vocabularies. The writings of Luke, for instance, are just what one would expect from a medical doctor, while John writes in a fisherman's language. It would appear then that they were not mere passive instruments or secretaries. Their personalities entered into the production of their books, and left definite indications in the results. A theory of inspiration must make allowance for such human characteristics.[8]

Most new evangelicals seem to hold the view of inspiration which has been identified above as verbal. The inspiring by the Holy Spirit was, to be sure, properly the inspiration of the writer, and can only derivatively be predicated on his writings as the result he produced under the Holy Spirit's influence. As such, the communication was of ideas or thought; but to be expressed, those thoughts had to be clothed in words—and the thoughts implied definite words. Thus, the guidance extended to the writer's choice of terminology, and can properly be termed verbal inspiration.[9]

This view is based on the statements and usage of the Scripture by Christ Himself. Because His argument sometimes hinged on a specific word, or even a letter, it is held that authority (which depends upon inspiration) extends even to words.

But isn't this dictation? If God so controlled the Scripture writer that each word he chose was precisely that which God would have him write, and no other, is this not tantamount to saying that God dictated the language to the writer? The new evangelicals are emphatic, even vehement, in their denial. While it may well be that the Bible contains instances of dictation, that was certainly not the norm. Because liberals had frequently accused conservatives of holding that the Bible had been dictated, the new evangelicals' explanation of this process is of considerable importance.

God's dealing with the prophet or apostle did not simply begin at the moment he sat down to write. Rather, God, who is in control of all things, had been at work from the man's birth and even before, preparing him. His birth into a given family, with the particular cultural influences which were brought to bear upon him, was no accident. His schooling, occupation, experiences, were all directed by the hand of God. Thus, his ways of thinking and reacting, his vocabulary—in short, the kind of person that he was—were the outcome of God's providence. In expressing a certain thought, the writer would characteristically employ a particular word. Yet that word, while his, would also be God's word. God, by a process somewhat analogous to mental telepathy, guided his thoughts as he wrote.

While this would seem to allow room for an independent choice of words, the issue is not quite so simple. In the expression of a given thought, there is not an unlimited possibility of available words. The thought of a ship will not be adequately expressed and preserved by the word "cow," for instance. A given thought implies a certain circle of words which are suitable to express it. If a thought is sufficiently precise, it may well be that there is only one word which will adequately convey its meaning. Thus, thoughts cannot be separated from words—the real issue is the precision of the thoughts.[10]

Not all the thoughts involved in the Biblical revelation are necessarily specific or detailed. Just as a picture may contain either much or little detail, but may be sharply focused or fuzzy, so the thought may sometimes have been rather general; nevertheless, it was a specific thought and no other that was involved.

But does not such inspiration still lead to dictation? Sometimes a secretary will become so well acquainted with her boss's ways of thinking and expressing himself that he has only to give her the rough outlines of a reply and she can compose the letter exactly as he would have written it.

If she really understands his thinking, she can actually anticipate his opinion, even though he may never have expressed himself on a particular point in her hearing. She thinks his thoughts, writes his words.

Here is how the new evangelicals conceive of verbal inspiration: God has worked in the life of the apostle or prophet, making him the kind of person that he is, possessing the vocabulary that God wanted him to have. The man lives in such a close relationship to God as to be very sensitive to His working. Then God, through the Holy Spirit, moves in his mind, directing and creating thoughts, and in a very precise fashion. So the man writes, using the words that God would have him use, yet without any consciousness of dictation. It seems that the evangelicals hold to verbal inspiration just as definitely as did the fundamentalists before them, but they have been concerned to analyze exactly what the term means and implies.[11]

One possible variant is the view of Bernard Ramm, as expressed in *Special Revelation and the Word of God,* where he cites with approval the statement of Shedd that the relationship between thoughts and words is dynamic or flexible. The same meaning may be expressed in different ways—direct or indirect discourse, and active or passive voice—and such phenomena do occur in the Gospels. Some have seen in this a denial of verbal inspiration. Read in its context, however, what Ramm is suggesting is that the same thought could have been (and, indeed, was) expressed in more than one way. He is not denying that God did actually choose these exact words.[12]

EVIDENCE OF SUPERNATURAL REVELATION

This, then, is the claim which the Bible makes for itself: that it is not merely the product of human intelligence, but that God Himself has made its content known to men, and supernaturally directed them in the recording of this knowledge. But what evidence is there that the claim is true? If there were some characteristics of the Bible which could not be accounted for simply on the basis of human authorship, they would argue for a supernatural origin.

One of the most prominent features of the Bible is prophecy. Ability to predict the contingent future is not ordinarily man's. While scientists may succeed in predicting events in a causal connection, historical events are not ordinarily susceptible to prognosis.

As an undergraduate, the writer once took a history course in which one century was examined in detail. The century was studied in thirds, and at the end of each third there was an examination. At the second exam, the question was: "On the basis of what transpired during the second third of the century, predict what you would expect to have happened during the last third, in the areas of art, politics, religion, etc." The graduate students in the class did rather poorly, for they had knowledge of what *did* actually happen during the period, and it was not at all what would have been expected.

The Bible contains numerous instances of genuine fulfilled prophecy.[18] Repeatedly Matthew says, "This was done that it might be fulfilled which was spoken by the prophet. . . ."

Some general observations need to be made regarding Biblical prophecy. First, the predictive aspect is merely secondary—the primary purpose of prophecy is the declaration of a message from God. The foretelling is subservient to the forthtelling. Prophecy pervades the entire Bible, not just being found in certain specifically "prophetical" books. Further, real prophecy is actually peculiar to the Bible. While prophecy may appear in other religions, it is found as only an occasional phenomenon, whereas it is part and parcel of Biblical religion.

Several objections raised against the argument for prophecy, must be considered and answered. One is that the language of Biblical prophecy is vague and general. If such were the case, it would not be difficult to find "fulfillments" of the prophecy.

The writer once attended a spiritualist meeting with three college friends. We decided to break up, two going in one door, the others coming in later through another door and sitting on the opposite side. After some preliminary predictions about world events, weather, and the like, the medium proceeded to make prophecies about specific individuals in the room. As she came to each person, she would close her eyes, rub her forehead, and utter an oracle. Coming to two of the college students, she said, "I see that you two young men are with the other two young men over there. You are doing something together, working together or going to school together."

The four of us left, not greatly impressed; because we were the only persons in the room under about fifty years of age (except for one teen-age girl), the deduction was not too difficult to make. General statements such as, "A great power will arise and will cause much evil," are fairly easy to make, since sooner or later there will almost certainly be some combination of events which will fit the description.

To be sure, some Biblical prophecies are of a rather general nature. This is not to say that they are therefore not of supernatural origin, but merely that they cannot be *demonstrated* to be supernatural. The first Messianic prophecy, found in Genesis 3:15, is scarcely specific. But some predictions are very explicit—the birthplace of the Messiah, the events of Palm Sunday, and the circumstances of Jesus' death are examples.

A second objection is that the prophecies are artificially fulfilled. A person knowing of a prophecy may deliberately bring about the circumstances predicted, and then claim fulfillment. Perhaps the prophet himself might precipitate the events which he has announced.

Again, this could be possible in the case of certain prophecies. Jesus might have fulfilled the Palm Sunday prophecy by acquiring the colt of an ass and riding it into Jerusalem (although there would be some difficulties, such as obtaining consent of the owner, and riding an unbroken colt). Some prophecies cannot be disposed of so easily, however. How could a single individual bring about the events connected with the Babylonian captivity and the return from exile? Similarly, some of the predicted circumstances connected with the crucifixion of Jesus were brought about by Roman soldiers, who probably had no knowledge of the prophecies and no motivation for wanting to see them fulfilled.

Finally, the critic sometimes objects on the basis that the

writing which prophesies the event actually was produced after the occurrence of the event "predicted." There was no difficulty in prophesying it then; it was simply a matter of describing what had been observed, which scarcely requires supernatural powers.

To be sure, there are books and passages whose date is in doubt. Without getting into the involved matter of "higher criticism" and the dating of the Biblical books, however, the force of the argument can still be sustained. Ramm constructs his case using only those passages which even the liberal dating accorded by the *International Critical Commentary* places before the fulfillment. And again, while the objection may apply to some instances of prophecy, it does not eliminate all. When all of these criticisms have been taken into account, there are still a considerable number of prophecies which Ramm is able to cite as evidently being of supernatural origin, employing the minor prophets. One of these may serve as an instructive example.

The Book of Nahum predicts and describes the destruction of the city of Nineveh, one prophecy which the *International Critical Commentary* does not consider to have been written after the event. It is very precise, detailed, and graphic. Consequently, its fulfillment is impressive. The city of Nineveh was a wealthy, well-fortified, populous city. At the very peak of its military and economic strength, Nahum predicted its destruction. The Medes attacked and besieged it. There was a river running through the city and when the river flooded, it washed away part of the wall, enabling the attackers to pour into the city, sack it, and burn it. Notice the several very specific predictions in the passage.

Nahum 1:10 says that the Ninevites would be devoured

while drunken. Believing that the Medes had been repulsed, the Ninevites prematurely began to celebrate, and in this drunken state were easily destroyed.

There are several references to the flood which played such an important part in the outcome of the battle. Nahum 1:8 (KJV) speaks of an "overrunning flood," and 2:6 (KJV) says, "The gates of the rivers shall be opened, and the palace shall be dissolved." The totality of the defeat is described in a number of ways. Chapter 3:3 (KJV) speaks of the number of persons who perished; 3:13 (KJV) tells of the fire that razed the city; 3:19 (KJV) speaks of the utter ruin, and Nineveh did cease to exist as a world power. Chapter 3:11 (KJV) says, ". . . thou shalt be hid." Nineveh was hid under mounds, and had to be excavated.

Many other instances of prophetic fulfillment could be offered. The argument is cumulative—as passage after passage is examined, the conviction increases that a supernatural intelligence and force have been at work producing these writings.

Yet another characteristic of the Bible leads us to suspect that it is of more than merely natural character. The very influence, or energy, of the Bible is such as to distinguish it as the most unusual of all books.

The Bible has enjoyed an amazing circulation. No book, ancient or modern, has had such a consistent popularity. It has enjoyed wide usage despite concerted and persistent opposition and attack. Particularly with the rise of historical or "higher" criticism, it has been subjected to minute analysis. Yet it has not been set aside as obsolete, but continues to be a best-seller.

Voltaire, who was opposed to much that the Bible

taught, once predicted that in a hundred years there would be no Bibles. One hundred years later, the house in which Voltaire had made that statement was owned by a Bible society and was used for storing Bibles. Voltaire's press was being used for the printing of Bibles.

The Bible has made a great impact on culture as well. How impoverished would be our English literature if all the references inspired by Biblical statements and Biblical themes were removed! Significant, indeed, is the influence of the Bible on law. In philosophy, politics, ethics, and art the Bible has also played a significant role. Consider the quality of the Bible's internal content. Where in the literature of other religions does one find anything to equal the Lord's Prayer or the discourse on holiness found in the Sermon on the Mount? Surely the Bible must be considered the most remarkable of all books.[14]

When one considers such data, he is faced with a decision. How will he account for the Bible's place? Will he say that it is the product of the highest human genius, a book written by means of the keenest insight of man? Or will he hold that this is because the Bible was written by men under a supernatural influence of the Holy Spirit? The new evangelicals unequivocally and resoundingly choose the second alternative. The Bible's own claims regarding its origin, nature, and authority are supported by its influence and phenomena.

The Witness of the Spirit

Actually, the conviction that the Bible is the Word of God does not rest upon any of these evidences. Theologically, it stems from the internal witness of testimony of the Holy Spirit, who certifies to the heart the divinity of the Scriptures, illuminates its meaning, and convicts the person of truth. Ramm has particularly developed this conception in *The Pattern of Religious Authority,* and at even greater length in *The Witness of the Spirit.*[15] He follows basically in the theological tradition established by John Calvin.

The big question, as Calvin saw it, was: If we accept the Bible as our authority because it is the Word of God, on what basis do we do so? Why do we take it to be the Word of God, other than the fact that it makes this claim for itself?

The Roman Catholic Church maintained that the church by its authority certified the divine origin of the Bible. However, one must first accept the authority of the church, and that view Calvin could not espouse. Too, there were those who sought to establish the inspiration of the Bible by the employment of rationalistic proofs. While Calvin does address himself to this matter in a section of his *Institutes,* he feels that these proofs from prophecy or miracle have value as a confirmation to the believer, *following* the sealing and convicting work of the Holy Spirit.

What, then, is the testimony of the Holy Spirit? It is not a religious experience of some great intensity. Nor is it a revelation in which some new truth is communicated which had not previously been possessed.

The Bible, as it is, is objectively the Word of God and is objectively true. Unfortunately, however, the unbeliever does not see or recognize that such is the case. Indeed, he is unable to understand or grasp the true significance of Scripture because of the effect of sin upon his thinking. As a man reads the Scripture, perhaps a passage that he has read or heard many times before, the Holy Spirit gives him *illumination*. He comes to understand the meaning of the passage and thus also comes to recognize the truth of it. There is assurance of truthfulness, or plenitude of conviction. This testimony, or witness, to God's truth is not limited to the truth in written form. It occurred prior to the reduction of the revelation to writing. It occurs also in connection with song, sermon, sacrament, or testimony.

Such witness ought not to be thought of as the communication of some information or new truth, but rather as an action of the Holy Spirit whereby the person becomes capable of understanding the truth already present. It is not as if the Holy Spirit told the individual that "the Bible is God's Word." That would be communication of information. It is rather an illuminating work of the Holy Spirit, enabling the reader to comprehend the word and to intuit its truth. As such, it is also a persuasion; it is primarily directed toward Jesus Christ and His gospel.

The principle of religious authority, Ramm would insist, is broader than some Protestants have made it—it is not simply the Bible *per se,* but the Holy Spirit speaking through the Bible. The two are not to be separated. Whereas the "enthusiasts" had looked to a direct message from the Holy Spirit, and Protestant scholastics (and later fundamentalism) had rested upon the Bible apart from the Spirit's illuminating work, Ramm combines them. He affirms that the Bible is the Word of God and is therefore true objectively; that is, whether or not anyone is reading and understanding it. It only functions effectually as the Word, however, when the Holy Spirit inwardly addresses it to the human understanding.

What is the relationship of testimony to the *indicia,* those features of the Bible that evidence is divinity? It is as the Holy Spirit illumines the mind of the individual that he recognizes the relevance of these, or sees them in their proper perspective. Without the Spirit's working, however, the evidences fail to convince the unbeliever.

THE TRUTHFULNESS OF SCRIPTURE

Certain other issues arise from the conception of inspiration. One is the truthfulness of Scripture, or, as it is sometimes termed, the inerrancy. The factors involved are rather simple: If the Bible is really the Word of God, then it would seem that it must be completely true in all of its teachings.

The new evangelicals hold that the Bible is entirely the Word of God. Such has been the effect of the inspiration by the Holy Spirit that every word is exactly what God would have had the Scripture writer to pen. If God is truly omniscient, then He could not make a mistake in what He communicated. If He is omnipotent, He is capable of transmitting His message and of having it recorded without the introduction of any errors. If He is completely truthful and benevolent, He would not have allowed any preventable errors to creep into the record. So, while the Bible does not itself explicitly claim freedom from error, this is a corollary, or an implication, of its view of inspiration. It is a conclusion to which believers have been driven as a result of their study of the doctrine of Scripture.

This view presents some difficulties. Certain statements in the Bible, or "phenomena of Scripture," seem to challenge the Bible's complete accuracy. A notable example is a series of apparent contradictions in parallel accounts in the Books of Kings and Chronicles. Where II Samuel 8:4 lists 700 horsemen, I Chronicles 18:4 numbers 7,000. Whereas II Samuel 10:18 says that David destroyed 700 Syrian chariots, I Chronicles 19:18 sets the figure at 7,000. In II Samuel 24:9, there are said to have been 800,000 men of Israel and 500,000 men of Judah, but I Chronicles 21:5 speaks of 1,100,000 and 470,000, respectively.

Other problems present themselves. Some Biblical statements appear to be in contradiction to what we now know from science. The excavation of certain Biblical sites raises some question as to whether some towns could actually have had the number of inhabitants attributed to them in the Scripture. The Gospel of Mark (6:8) has Jesus allowing the disciples to take a staff, whereas according to Matthew 10:10 and Luke 9:3, a staff was prohibited. These and numerous other items in the Scripture would seem to conflict with the claim that the Bible is free from error.

The problem of inerrancy is simply one of reconciling two types of considerations: the Bible's teachings regarding its inspiration, and the Bible's characteristics or the result of inspiration. Approaches which emphasize the former and seek to harmonize the phenomena of Scripture to the doctrine are generally referred to as "deductive," while those which begin with an examination of the actual characteristics of the Bible and seek to determine what sort of inspiration would have produced such work are termed "inductive." The new evangelicals appear to be attempting a course between these two poles. They derive their doctrine of inspiration from the teaching of the Bible itself, yet maintain that the inductive difficulties must be taken seriously, and an effort made to resolve them.

A number of men have dealt with the issues involved here. Perhaps the major amount of effort has been that expended by Everett F. Harrison, professor of New Testament at Fuller Theological Seminary.[16] He is insistent that thorough study must be made of the nature of Biblical truthfulness. Exactly what does it mean to say that the Bible is free from error? What would constitute an error?

Certain general guidelines emerge from Harrison's study. Perhaps all of them could be seen as beginning with the statement that the Bible must be interpreted and judged in terms of its own usage and intentions, and by the standards of meaning and accuracy employed in its day, rather than by twentieth-century standards.

We should note first that when the Bible speaks of natural matters, it is using phenomenal language rather than scientifically precise language. It simply describes an event the way it would appear to the human eye. Thus the sun is described as "rising" and "setting" because that is how it appears to the eye. No error is involved here. Actually, we find a parallel in present usage, also. When the weatherman on television says, "The sun rose at 6:33 A.M. today and will set at 5:45 P.M.," the station isn't flooded with calls protesting that the weatherman made a scientific error.

Nor is the Bible's use of numbers and time very specific, in many cases. Jesus never met anyone at 3:20 or at 10 minutes before five. It was always the third hour or the sixth hour, because time was thought of, in that culture, in terms of three-hour blocks. To demand closer specification of time would be to interpret the Bible in a fashion foreign to its cultural setting, and thus to treat it unfairly. The same principle operates in certain areas of our culture. If I earned $12,104.02 last year (a purely hypothetical case), it would usually be deemed correct to say in ordinary conversation that I made $12,000. When filling in my Form 1040, however, I had better be a bit more specific, although even the Internal Revenue Department will now allow me to round to the even dollar. Truth must be judged in the context of usage.

We must also seek to get at the exact meaning of a term. If the Bible speaks of someone as a son, it may not mean a male first-generation descendent, but simply one possessing certain qualities. Numerous other examples could be given.

The purpose in view and the audience being addressed also frequently governed the language, and the Scripture should be evaluated and judged in terms of those factors. A change by Luke of "Hosanna in the highest" to "Glory in the highest" needs to be appraised in the light of *Hosanna* being a Semitic word which would not have been understood by Luke's Gentile readers. He therefore substituted an equivalent expression, which ought not to be charged as an error.

Finally, we ought to note that the Bible is a progressive revelation. The degree of completeness and exactness was proportional to the degree of spiritual maturity of the recipients of the revelation. Early passages consequently do not give the same amount of detail as later portions.

Perhaps all of these statements can be summarized by saying that many of the apparent errors in Scripture appear erroneous because of a misunderstanding of what Scripture involves. When more stringent demands are placed upon it than are appropriate to its nature and purpose, it will seem to contain mistakes.

Effort must be made to resolve the difficulties, of course. Harrison proceeds to examine some of the troublesome items of Scripture, many of which, he observes, can be adequately explained. The science of archaeology has been of great help. Some of the difficulties of a hundred years ago present no difficulty now. Once it was alleged that the Bible was seriously in error in its reference to Sargon (Isaiah 20:1), since secular history of the region knew nothing of such a person. When archaeology uncovered emphatic evidence of the existence of Sargon, it was the Bible, rather than its critics, that was vindicated.

Other seeming contradictions also vanish when examined closely. Matthew speaks of two demoniacs (Matthew 8:28), two blind men (Matthew 20:30), two animals (Matthew 21:2-7), whereas the other accounts have only one in each case. Conversely, Luke speaks of two angels at Christ's tomb, whereas Matthew and Mark mention only one. Note, however, that in no case does the account which speaks of one say that there was one *and only one*. Thus, the seeming contradiction may again be an instance of selection for emphasis.

We do not presently see the solution of all the problems. It may be that further evidence will resolve the difficulty, as it has in other areas. In some cases the necessary information may have been lost so that the solution will not appear. The trend, however, has been toward alleviating the problems and, consequently, based on the Bible's teaching regarding its own inspiration, we can continue to hold it to be free from error.

Another possible solution to the problem is suggested by Edward Carnell.[17] He notes the genuine difficulties attaching to certain of the "phenomena." The conflicting records in the accounts of Kings and Chronicles come in for special attention. How are these to be regarded and treated?

Carnell observes that the mere presence of a given statement in Scripture does not guarantee its truth. Inspiration only assures us that this is what the speaker named actually did assert. The statements of Job's "friends," for example, are not true and infallible simply because they stand recorded in the Bible. Similarly, the statement, "There is no God" (Psalm 14:1, KJV) is not a truth. What is true is that "the fool hath said in his heart, There is no God." Inspiration, in at least some cases, merely guarantees that the writer was preserved from error in recording what may well have been an erroneous statement.

In similar fashion Carnell then asks about Stephen's speech prior to his stoning (Acts 7). His statement about Abram leaving Haran after the death of his father, Terah (v. 4) seems to conflict with Genesis 11:26 and 32, and 12:4. What is to be made of this? Carnell states that unless we are ready to maintain that Stephen as he spoke was under the inspiration of the Holy Spirit, we can only say that this is truly and accurately what Stephen said, and not that what he said must necessarily be true.

Can this principle be extended further? Carnell feels that, if necessary, it could be carried to the problem of conflicting accounts in Samuel and Chronicles. Perhaps one (or both) of the writers had an inaccurate source document before him as he wrote. Inspiration might merely have meant that he copied correctly the source which he was using, involving even the incorporation of errors. It would not have meant that he was guided to correct the errors found in the sources. While Carnell does not say that he personally follows this approach, or that he feels compelled to adopt such an expedient, he acknowledges it as a definite possibility.

A difficulty can be seen in this method of treating the problem. If inspiration only produced correct records of what may be erroneous accounts, one can only be certain of the correctness of Biblical statements where (1) he can be certain that no source was involved in the writing of the document; or (2) he knows on independent grounds that it is true. Carnell feels that theology is not threatened by this, since it comes from Romans and Galatians, which Paul received by direct revelation. Other portions cannot be disposed of so easily, and it may be awareness of these difficulties which has prevented Carnell and others from adopting the solution.

One further possibility has been suggested by Daniel P. Fuller, dean of Fuller Theological Seminary. In a paper read before the Evangelical Theological Society on December 27, 1967, he emphasized that the main purpose of the Bible is to make men wise unto salvation. He observes that the verses which are cited as teaching the inerrancy of the Scriptures deal with such matters. Inerrancy cannot be extended beyond that. In order to communicate His truth in revelational matters most adequately, God accommodated Himself in nonrevelational matters to the way the original readers viewed the world about them.

CONCLUSIONS

Having followed the new evangelical theology through this discussion of the crucial area of Biblical authority, let us recapitulate. Just what is the nature and the function of the Bible for these theologians?

God, who is unlimited, perfect, and supremely wise, is not knowable by man's own effort. So high is He above man that the latter really cannot grasp Him, but God has made Himself known in certain general ways to all men through nature and within the heart of man. In addition, God has taken the initiative in specially making Himself known within man's experience. There are several varieties of His special revelation: His speech or verbal communication, His acts in history, and, most fully, the actual coming of Jesus into the human race. Because God is the supreme Almighty Creator and Ruler of the human race, His words and actions have binding authority upon man. He has the right to prescribe belief and practice.

In order that the value of this revelation might not be lost with the ceasing of the actual revealing activity, and so that God would not have to continue to give the revelation repeatedly, He has preserved it by causing it to be recorded in written form. This He did by the Holy Spirit's exercising on

certain men an influence termed "inspiration." It was of
such a nature that, as they recorded what had been revealed, their writings were exactly what God wanted written. These Scriptures are, when properly interpreted, completely free from error in their assertions. The Book is actually God's Word to men.

The Bible is not an end in itself. Its value is instrumental:
it is intended to bring the reader into a certain relationship
with the God who stands behind it. It is never to be rever-
enced or worshiped, and it is not to be conceived of as
having some magical or automatic effect.[18]

There is, in other words, an additional element involved
in the Bible's functioning as an authority: namely, "illumination." The ultimate authority is the Holy Spirit
speaking in the Word. As the Bible is read, the Holy Spirit
works in such a way as to bring to the reader an understanding of the Word, and thus a conviction of its truth. There is
a pattern of authority, the written Word (external) and the
witness of the Spirit (internal) together constituting the
voice of God.

In what ways does this conception of Biblical revelation
differ from that of neo-orthodoxy? Some have suggested
that the new evangelicals' view is not in any essential respect different from that of Karl Barth or Emil Brunner.

Neo-orthodoxy says that revelation is an active process.
God does not reveal information about Himself, or give
divine propositions. Revelation is God presenting Himself.
To the neo-orthodox, the Bible is not itself the Word of
God; it is merely a record of the occasion of revelation. It
may become the Word of God when, as one is exposed to it

through reading or preaching, he encounters God. It is this encounter itself, however, which is the revelation. Without the special "spark," as it were, supplied by God, the Bible is lifeless, says the neo-orthodox theologian.

While there are many points of similarity and difference between neo-orthodoxy and the new evangelicalism, one major area clearly separates the two theologies. According to the new evangelicals, the Bible is objectively the Word of God whether anyone is reading or hearing it, and whether one is actually encountering God in the Bible or not. This is stressed in a number of ways. Ramm says that the Bible is divine revelation in written form. Its words are, when properly understood, what God would actually have man to know, understand, and do.

If, however, the truth being impressed upon the heart—illumination—is the same subjective experience that the neo-orthodox calls revelation, is there not merely a difference of terminology between the two? Typically the experience is something like this: A person is reading the Bible, perhaps even a very familiar portion. It does not particularly affect or stir him. He is comparatively unmoved. Then he is gripped by the passage; it seems to speak to him. He is jarred by something meaningful, affected by a spiritual reality. Or he may be listening to a sermon with some degree of interest, when suddenly the words pertain to *him*. They are no longer merely universal truths.

For the neo-orthodox, God does not say something, communicate some information—the encounter itself is the revelation. The new evangelical insists that the words are objectively true and that, correctly understood, they have

one definite meaning. Illumination conveys understanding
of the meaning and persuasion as to its truth. Presumably
this meaning would be the same for anyone receiving the
illumination. Also, once one has had the illumination, the
understanding would be retained, dependent, of course,
upon memory, although the same intensity or vividness may
not persist. In the neo-orthodox view, however, since there
is no definite revealed content of an informational character, one does not retain some message from the revelation-
situation. One does not have a revealed truth which he may
repeat to others. He can only point others in the direction of
the revelation-encounter. God may encounter different persons quite differently through the same text of the Bible, or
even the same person on different occasions.[19]

The new evangelical, in common with other conservatives, can therefore quote the Bible with a sense that this is
what God actually intends man to know. The problem of
determining the meaning may be still present, but at least
there is an objective truth.

III

The Doctrinal Content

In examining the doctrinal structure of the new evangelicalism, one feels a certain frustration. It is difficult to construct a comprehensive system of doctrine for the movement, but not because the new evangelicals are not systematic, or because they go around with fragments of a theology with large gaps in between.

The new evangelicalism holds much of its theology in common with fundamentalism and other orthodox theology. It has therefore not spoken out in some of these areas. It is where fundamentalism has seemed to distort the correct understanding, or where new data has been discovered, or where new problems now face the orthodox theologian, that the new evangelicals have articulated their doctrinal views. Their writings have primarily dealt with certain problem areas, rather than constituting a complete systematic theology (although there is a pressing need for an up-to-date conservative systematic theology text). The closest approximation to a systematic theology is a series of articles by various writers which first appeared in *Christianity Today* and has since been printed in a volume entitled *Basic Christian Doctrines*. Not all of the contributors to this book could be classified as new evangelicals, however, nor is it really a comprehensive theological work. Nonetheless, distinctive contributions have been made by the new evangelicals in several areas, although they nowhere approximate the complete and detailed treatment accorded the doctrine of revelation.

GOD

The knowledge of God has been under intense study in the twentieth century. We have already seen that the new evangelicals hold that the Bible, as a special revelation, gives us a knowledge of God's nature and will. Is there any other basis for knowledge of Him? Is there a natural knowledge of God outside of the Bible? What is its extent and quality? [1]

Some have maintained that it is possible to formulate some knowledge of God on the basis of philosophy, apart from the Bible or a prior commitment of faith. This approach, known as "natural theology," is best represented by the classical proofs or arguments for the existence of God, according to which one can at least know that there is a God. While classical liberalism made much of natural theology, Barthianism emphatically rejected any natural theology. Older orthodox theologies frequently included it in an earlier section entitled "Theism."

One of the major arguments is the cosmological, in which a man looks about himself at the world and says, in effect, "Where did it come from?" Since it would appear that the world could not be its own cause, there must somewhere be an ultimate cause, a being which is absolutely independent, not requiring anything else for its existence.

A second argument is the teleological, or design, which contends that when one examines the universe, he detects what appears to be a remarkable *order* in it. Man is able to live because there is an atmosphere made up of certain proportions of various elements: if these proportions were slightly altered, man could not live; if the atmosphere were slightly heavier, man would be crushed. Man possesses intricate eyes, enabling him to see. If one found a watch with all of its carefully ordered mechanism, he would assume that it had not just happened to be; it had been made by some intelligent watchmaker. Similarly, the orderliness of the universe and its occupants suggests that some intelligence must have been at work, ordering or designing the world in this special fashion.

Finally, there is the moral or anthropological argument. Man has a sense of "ought," a compulsion that he should do certain things because they are right and avoid other actions because they are wrong. How does one justify such conceptions, however? There must be an objective norm for ethical judgment; that is, a standard which goes beyond the likes and dislikes of individuals. This, in turn, would require a moral law-giver.

The natural theologian believes that the three arguments have a cumulative effect. Each adds some further data to the conception of God. The first indicates His power and creative ability, the second shows His intelligence, while the third establishes His moral character.

For a long time, these proofs were considered valid by theologians. Thomas Aquinas, probably the outstanding natural theologian in the whole history of the church, formulated a fivefold proof for the existence of God, based on the philosophy of Aristotle. The Thomistic natural theology is still officially held by the Roman Catholic Church.

The theistic arguments came under heavy criticism in the eighteenth century and after, as indicated in the opening chapter of this work. As blow after blow fell upon them, they gradually crumbled. In the twentieth century, the teachings of logical positivism and ordinary language analysis, and, from another direction, existentialism, completed the task. For most philosophers today, the proofs are largely unconvincing. Natural or rational knowledge of God is in a rather poor state.

To some theologians, this has been a catastrophe, but the new evangelicals have seen the development differently. Far from being destructive of faith, it has helped to direct attention back to the true source of knowledge of God. The evangelicals hold that the primary datum is Biblical revelation, and that philosophical evidences are secondary and supportive. The way of natural theology was, in their opinion, largely a blind pathway by which theologians placed trust in natural reason, to the neglect of revelation. When reason then went on to reject the proofs for God, it was assumed that the case for theism had perished with them.

There is a danger in basing a good belief upon a poor reason. It is something like the foolish man in Jesus' parable who built his house upon the sand, and when the storm came, not only the sand was washed away, but the house, also. So, the case for theism having rested largely upon the theistic arguments, belief in God suffered unnecessarily.[2]

Note again that the fault lies in man himself. The failure is a result of man's sin, distorting the revelation of God in nature. That seemingly all men have some religion is testimony to a valid general revelation, but the great diversity of religions appears to be evidence that this general revelation is not efficacious for man as we find him.

Man cannot discover God. Even the knowledge of God is of grace, for God is known only where and as He has chosen to make Himself known. He maintains the initiative. This is not to say that there is no abiding knowledge of Him now, but simply to say that it came only by God's origination. The self-manifestation of God was progressive: like a parent educating a child, God gradually disclosed more of His nature and will as the human race grew in its ability to comprehend spiritual truth. The law constituted the fundamentals of the knowledge of God. More advanced truth came in the prophetical writings. In Jesus Christ, however, the very presence of God most fully made Him known. Here was doctrine not merely declared; it was doctrine demonstrated.

What is this God like? What has been revealed about Him? The Bible does not speak much of God in abstract fashion, perhaps partly because the Hebrew mind was not much inclined toward abstractions. Instead of citing the omnipotence of God, Jesus said, after comparing the difficulty of a rich man entering the Kingdom of God to a camel going through the eye of a needle, "But with God all things are possible." Instead of declaring the omniscience of God,

Jesus said, ". . . the very hairs of your head are all numbered" (Matthew 10:30, KJV). Instead of a discussion of
the providence of God, the Twenty-third Psalm says, "The
Lord is my shepherd, I shall not want."

God is not treated in abstract fashion. He is described
primarily in His relationship to man. He is personal and self-
communicating. Many of the statements of theologians
about the nature of God are inferences and, while legitimate, should not change our conception of the basic nature
and purpose of revealed theological knowledge. God's revelation was not given simply to supply information about
Himself; it was to enable man to become properly related to
God.

Perhaps the two most prominent attributes of God in the
Biblical revelation are His love and His holiness. A major
problem in the doctrine of God has traditionally been the
relation of these two attributes. How can God be both loving and holy? If He really loves man, why doesn't He just
forgive his sins? Why does the "pound of flesh" have to be
exacted from someone? How can a loving God consign
anyone to a hell, a place of endless suffering? On the other
hand, if God is really righteous and holy, how can He allow
anyone to enter into heaven without having to work for his
salvation? How can there be such a thing as salvation by
pure grace?

So opposed do these qualities seem that some have regarded them as virtually antithetical. There seems to be a
conflict within the nature of God. When one reads the
Bible, these two themes alternate, like the crash of thunder
on a stormy night and the sweet singing of birds on a peace-

ful sunny morning. One Scottish theologian, drawing his metaphor from the geography of his homeland, referred to the "stormy north side and the sunny south side of God." Some have gone even further. In the second century Marcion taught that there were two gods depicted in the Bible: the god of the Old Testament, a being of righteousness and wrath, and the New Testament god, characterized by love, gentleness, and benevolence.

Some theologies have emphasized one attribute to the neglect of the other. Extreme forms of Calvinism tended to place so much weight on God's holiness and righteousness that love and mercy were somewhat atrophied. God, for His own glory, saves whom He will and damns whom He will, in a rather arbitrary fashion.

In recent liberal theology the tendency has been to emphasize God's love. At times this has been carried to the point of actually making Him somewhat indulgent. God overlooks departures from His will. He does not require recompense or restitution for sin. In its extreme forms, this has sometimes been wryly characterized by Calvinists as the doctrine of the "grandfatherhood of God." Frequently it leads to a universalism. Because a loving father would not condemn anyone to endless suffering, all must ultimately be saved.

The new evangelicals have insisted, however, that there is no internal conflict in God's nature. Far from being opposed, these two attributes can only be adequately and fully understood when taken in conjunction with one another. They are not like two colors which clash with one another, such as orange and red. They are more like two complementary colors, such as blue and yellow, which accentuate one another. We get into difficulty when we start from two poles and try to work inward, defining the concepts somewhat abstractly; they then frequently conflict. Rather, we ought to recognize that whatever God's love and holiness are, they are capable of coexisting harmoniously, for they do in God. God is not pictured in Scripture as a Jekyll and Hyde struggling within Himself. We should start from the center, the unified personality of God, and work toward a definition of the attributes.

Love can only be completely understood or measured when seen in conjunction with the divine holiness. It is best discerned as grace, God's free gift of salvation. Grace is only meaningful, however, in light of the holiness of God, which requires the provision of atonement. The great holiness of God means that He cannot simply accept man as he is. Some sort of restitution must be made for this deviation from God's perfect holiness, which constitutes sin. God's holiness requires that He not simply sweep sin under the rug, forgetting about it. The love of God is seen, however, in His making this provision Himself.

The God of Scripture is the Rescuer, the Ransomer, the Redeemer of man. The measure of the greatness of His love is how much He has been willing to do. Holiness is properly estimated in view of the greatness of the sacrifice: the death of His own Son. The holiness of God does not compete with His love; it prevents it from degenerating into mere sentimentality. No modification of either quality is necessary or desirable.

Another major issue is the transcendence and immanence of God. Transcendence means that God is in some way separate from, above, or apart from the world and man. Immanence means that God is in some fashion present or active within the world and nature. Carl Henry believes that "in these days the problem of God revolves mainly around the dispute over divine transcendence and immanence." He feels that it touches virtually every crucial issue of traditional theology.

Liberal theology stressed God's immanence. God was seen as present within nature and carrying out His purposes from within it and by its processes. Evolution was a particularly suitable expression of God's indirect working. A convenient little motto was "Some call it evolution, others call it God." The liberal was not concerned about the cruciality of the virgin birth; to him every birth was a "miracle," a work of God. God was not merely present in the spectacular or unusual, but present in every occurrence. Further, God and man were seen as quite similar. God's moral standards were largely identified with man's highest ideals. Finally, liberalism believed that God could be known through nature and by man's powers of reason.

Fundamentalism made much of transcendence. God is the miracle-worker, intervening in nature. The miracles, and in particular the virgin birth, are important because they support the view of God as transcendent. There is a radical moral and spiritual separation between God and man. The holiness of God is not merely the goodness of man written in large capital letters, or pronounced in a loud voice. The struggle between fundamentalism and liberalism frequently turned upon this basic difference in the view of

God and His relation to the creation, although it was not always recognized.

The new evangelicals insist upon God's transcendence. He is not merely identified with this world's processes nor bound by its laws. Miracles have a genuine place in a theistic universe. God also is distinguished morally and spiritually from man. The holiness of God far surpasses the goodness of man.

At the same time immanence must not be neglected, as fundamentalism tended to do. God does work indirectly, or through "natural processes." This is seen in the concept of progressive creationism, to be examined later. It is also involved in the idea of God's general providence. When the new evangelical has a toothache, he does not ordinarily pray for a miraculous healing; he goes to the dentist. The fundamentalist, of course, also did this. It is the new evangelical who has more thoroughly worked out the theoretical basis behind it: that God has as genuinely worked through medical science as through a miracle of healing.

Similarly, the new evangelicalism tends to be more culture-affirming than was fundamentalism. God does work through even unregenerate man, and there is something to be learned from general culture.

The doctrine of the trinity has proved difficult throughout almost the entire history of Christianity. Even in orthodox circles, the view that God is both three and one has tended constantly to slip into one or the other error. Tritheism really conceives of three gods, like three men side by side. Modalism thinks of one God, manifesting Himself in three modes of existence, something like one actor playing three different roles in a play. The new evangelicals have sought to cling to both poles of this view.

We must take seriously, they would say, the Biblical emphasis upon the unity of God: He is one god, as Israel was taught to instruct its children. While this is most prominent within the Old Testament, it is found throughout the Bible. At the same time, the Bible speaks clearly of three as being divine. There seems to be some variety within the divine unity; there are personal distinctions within the godhead. This trinitarian monotheism is a disclosure of divine revelation. The parallels in non-revelational philosophy bear only a superficial resemblance to the Biblical doctrine.

The Old Testament contains certan intimations or foregleams of the doctrine of the trinity, such as the plural verb ("let us make") and possessive pronominal suffix ("in our image") with a singular subject and verb ("and God said") in Genesis 1:26. But it was with the full personal coming of Jesus Christ as Son that the trinity was fully disclosed.

The trinity is not simply a trinity of mode or function in which the Father is God in one activity, the Son is God functioning in another area and the Spirit is yet another dimension of the divine life and work. It is an ontological trinity. There are somehow three definite distinctions in the very being of God, yet in some way these three—Father, Son, and Holy Spirit—can all be said to be one. While this mystery is not comprehensible, these new evangelical theologians are careful to defend their view against the charge of being logically contradictory. They would insist that while God is one and three, He is not one and three in the same respect, which would be sheer logical contradiction.

The trinity, then, is a mystery, a term preferred to "paradox," or even the adjective "inscrutable" used by some earlier theologians. Every analogy falls short of explaining it. Even the figure drawn from the multiple personalities sometimes encountered in one person is rejected by Henry as implying a conflict within the personality of God. Perhaps the normal ability of a person to assume positions and represent various viewpoints in internal discussion (what Reinhold Niebuhr calls "the self in dialogue with itself") would be more helpful here. Usually, trying to give too concrete a meaning to the concept ends in a lapse into error in either one direction or the other.

Theology is not in a unique difficulty here, however. Physicists are not certain how to regard light. Some of its characteristics can be accounted for only by the theory that light is waves. Other qualities are best explained in the hypothesis that light is particles, or bundles, of energy. Scientists continue to hold both theories as being necessary to account for all of light's phenomena, yet light cannot be both. One physics major put it this way: "On Monday, Wednesday, and Friday we hold the wave theory; on Tuesday, Thursday, and Saturday we hold the corpuscular theory." (Evidently the physicist does not think about the nature of light on Sunday!) Yet the physicist does not cease to believe in light. While there are conspicuous differences, notably in epistemology, there is nonetheless a parallel here to the mystery of the trinity.

The trinity is of importance not simply because of its own status as a doctrine, but also because of its critical relationship to other significant doctrines. Henry maintains that deviation on such matters as supernatural regeneration, the incarnation, election, revelation, and atonement follows from prior rejection of the doctrine of the trinity, and becomes evident when the implications of that rejection are consistently carried out.

For example, some reject as immoral the substitutionary theory of the atonement. The idea that God should punish an innocent Person, Jesus, in place of guilty persons simply does not seem right. This might well be, if God and Jesus were totally separate. Henry contends, however, that in view of the doctrine of the trinity, this objection collapses. God does not take an innocent person who must voluntarily submit to the death of the cross. Jesus Christ is also God, as is the Father, and the decision that He should die on the cross was made by the triune God, although the Father executed the decision. The charge of immorality against the substitutionary view stems from a denial of the trinity: the idea that Jesus is not God, and is not somehow one with the Father.

MAN AND SIN

When we come to the doctrine of man, we enter an area of relevance broader than theology. Other disciplines may not concern themselves much with God or the future things, but man is the object of study by history and the social sciences, and even by natural science. There are therefore a number of non-Biblical materials and opinions bearing on man.

"What is man, that thou are mindful of him?" asks the

Psalmist (Psalm 8:4, KJV). It is to this question that the new evangelical theologian first directs his thinking: the nature of man.

Man is pictured in the Bible as being the creation of God. He has not come to be simply through the chance bumping together of atoms, or a process of natural selection. The Biblical description shows God making man by a definite and distinct act, not only in the classic creation account in Genesis, but in the poetic and prophetic books as well.

Just what did this creation involve? Did God directly create both the material aspect (the body) and the immaterial aspect (the soul) of man? The Biblical account implies that some pre-existing material was employed: " . . . then the Lord God formed man of dust from the ground, and breathed into his nostrils the breath of life; and man became a living being" (Genesis 2:7, RSV). Or did God make man from some pre-existing form of life? Might God have taken some living higher primate, and said in effect, "You're it," and done something or added something (a soul) to this form, making it qualitatively different and thus constituting him man?

For the most part, the evangelicals have taken the position that God's direct creation included not only man's soul, but his body as well. In attempting to take the Bible as directly as possible, they find that its description of man's origin seemingly implies direct creation. Yet, Carnell notes, this same Biblical text also seems to teach literal twenty-four-hour "days," a concept which has been abandoned because of considerations of geology. If necessary, the theistic evolutionary interpretation could be adopted, namely the idea that the "dust" referred to was an already existing form of life.

There is enough evidence for the evolution of man to make the evangelical cautious about making his pronouncement, but the evidence is far from compelling. These men are not about to adopt the position of theistic evolution with the scientific evidence in its present ambiguous condition. This would involve a revised view of the degree of assertion being made by the Bible in the creation account. At the same time, the evangelicals do not want to categorically close the door on any possible future data.[3]

Nor are these men dogmatic regarding the antiquity of man.[4] At one time it was held that the Biblical genealogies could be made to establish a date for the origin of the human race, a date set by Bishop Ussher at 4004 B.C. It would be an understatement indeed to say that this date conflicted with the views of anthropologists, some of whom dated man as old as one million years.

A closer examination of the text, however, has indicated that Ussher's conclusion was unwarranted. The genealogies evidently cannot be regarded as continuous lists of father-son descent. There apparently are gaps in the list; a given name may represent an entire clan, rather than just an individual. Hence the date need not be clung to, although there is some question as to just how much time can be absorbed into the lists.

Evangelical scholars are divided as to how to date Adam. Some, identifying him with early fossil man, allow a figure as high as a million years. Others, who place him at about

40,000 years, maintain either that earlier forms were not human or that they belong to some pre-Adamite race, of men. There are some difficulties in any of these interpretations, and for the most part, the evangelicals have left the exact dating of man an open issue.

Of greater importance is the unity of the human race.[5] Are all men descended from a common ancestor, or were there two or more streams of origin of the human race as we know it today? Again the fossil record gives some divergence of evidence.

Doctrinal significance is attached to this point. Paul argues in Romans 5 that all men are sinners and therefore are under condemnation. The reason is that in Adam sin entered the race, and all men are descended from Adam. Thus Paul's argument seems to stand or fall with the unity of the human race. If there are men who are not derived from Adam, they may not have Adam's sinful nature and his guilt, and therefore may not be in need of redemption.

The new evangelicals feel that abandoning the monogenetic theory could have far-reaching consequences for one's view of man, and for one's conception of Scripture. There is some paleontological evidence for the polygenetic view; yet this seems in recent years to be less impressive or weighty than that for the monogenetic claim. Ramm argues further that anatomically, physiologically, psychologically, and physically, the human race is one. Therefore he concludes that all men are descended from a common origin or from a single pair.

Just what is man? What is his makeup? [6] Recent theological thought has strongly stressed the unity of man. While agreeing with this, the new evangelicals would insist that, in addition to its material side, man's nature has an immaterial aspect, or a spiritual side, which is properly termed a "soul." Man is a unity and is only fully man when the two elements of his nature are joined into a sort of compound. Yet these two elements of his nature can still be broken down, like the elements of a chemical compound. This, indeed, happens at death. At the resurrection, the body in a changed form is reunited with the soul.

Animals as well as men have a psychic side to their being. Naturalism has traditionally maintained that man's soul is simply a more complex form of the psychic activity found in animals. While there is no denying that man and animal have this in common, the theologians would insist that psychic activity is not what Christian theology means by a soul.

The soul, rather, is that aspect of man's being which links him to a rational and moral supernatural realm. It is that by which he is able to relate to a personal God. It is that which distinguishes him most fully from other living creatures. Another way of putting it is to say that man, of all the creatures, has been created in the image of God, and bears this image, based upon statements such as Genesis 1:26 and 27. Determination of precisely what this means is our major task.

Historically, a strong tradition has stressed the rational element. This Graeco-Roman interpretation has made man's rational capacities virtually divine. The Hebrew-Christian tradition in large measure agrees with this conception, yet challenges it at several points. It is true that man's reason links him to a world of supernature, but this is not the full meaning of the image of God. There is a spiritual as well as a rational significance to the image. Furthermore, the Hebrew-Christian tradition asserted that even before the entrance of sin, human reason was dependent upon divine revelation, because of the great gulf between the infinite mind of God and the finite mind of man.

A major element in the image of God is the conscience, a rather formal factor that tells man that he ought to do what is right and love what is good. Originally it probably also included some positive content, some actual knowledge of good.

Certain of the characteristics, or capacities, of man make possible his religious relationship to God without their being specifically religious. Thus man, by virtue of being man, is capable of faith or trust. This capacity is exercised toward objects other than God, but still it is part of the endowment of man which can be termed "the image of God."

This image is not now found perfect and intact in man. The entrance of sin in the human race has modified and distorted, but not obliterated, it. Man's reason is now even less competent to receive and judge God's revelation. While man is not essentially evil, he also is not actually good. There is now a defect at the very center of man's spiritual makeup, so that he does not perfectly understand what is good, and does not desire to do it.

In their treatment of the image of God, the new evangelicals steer between two extremes. Roman Catholicism, following a lead set by Origen, drew a distinction between the image of God and the likeness of God, as found in the Biblical text. The image was the natural similarity to God —reason, freedom, and so forth—which was not affected by the fall. The likeness to God was a set of supernaturally added gifts, *e.g.* positive goodness, which *was* lost in the fall. This meant that man's ability to know and will was intact; he was capable of good deeds.

Some neo-orthodox theologians have almost made man inherently sinful. Not holding to a temporal fall, they have had to trace man's sinfulness to some originally created condition. The new evangelicals teach that man was indeed created sinless and innocent, but that early in the history of the human race, mankind sinned; the image was marred.

Any estimate of man as we find him presently constituted must give strong weight to the factor of sin. Man may have been God's perfect creation—sinless, pure, and like God— but man as a sinner would be a better way to describe him as we find him today.

What is sin? Is it a certain act? Is it thought or attitude? The new evangelicals consider sin to be any lack of conformity to God's moral and spiritual law, whether it is a matter of deed, word, thought, attitude, or disposition. Actively, it may be transgression of God's law, or going beyond the limits He has set. Passively, it may be "falling short," or failure to do what God desires and commands. It may be doing God's will but "not quite," such as performing an outwardly proper act, but with an improper motivation, as for selfish reasons.

Basically, sin seems to be man's tendency toward autonomy, rather than surrender of self, life, will to God. The essence of sin seems to be preferring the self before God, and in this sense sin can be said to be selfishness. It does not consist merely of discrete acts. It is an indwelling corruption of nature which is the source or principle of action. Sin is not necessarily to be identified with *conscious* sin. Man does not become a sinner when he sins; he sins because he is a sinner.

The sinful tendency in man shows itself in specific acts. No parent has ever had to teach a child selfishness. The newspaper on the day this passage is written tells of a young man murdering eight student nurses in Chicago; of racial riots; of a continuing war in Vietnam—outward expressions of the inward bent or distortion of man.

Another way of putting it is to say that man is "totally depraved." [7] Total depravity does not mean that sinners are as bad as they can possibly be—the man who beats his wife does not beat her all the time, and the person who cheats on his income tax does not cheat in every imaginable fashion, or steal at every opportunity. Nor does it mean that men cannot and do not perform any acts of general goodness—even the murderer may be a kind, thoughtful, and generous husband and father. It does mean that there is in the unbeliever no natural affection for God. The effect of sin permeates the entire nature of man. Furthermore, man cannot remedy this spiritual defect by the moral and spiritual power present within him. The best he can do is to express his pride and selfishness in more sophisticated and subtle fashions.

Depravity, or original sin, traces back to the beginning of the human race. The first human pair were placed on probation. They chose sin, putting their own wills above God. As a result, all men now begin life with a corrupted nature, inclined toward evil rather than good.

There is some difference of opinion as to how the primal sin of the human race could affect the descendants of Adam and Eve. For the most part the new evangelicals espouse the federal headship theory,[8] which holds that Adam acted as a representative. Because he sinned, sin and death came upon the entire human race, and men now begin their existence out of fellowship with God.

But is it fair that I should be held guilty of Adam's sin, and be punished for it, when I had nothing to say about it? Not only was it not my sin, but I did not even choose Adam to represent me. While a partial answer comes from the fact that each one has ratified Adam's sin by his own choice, this is still inadequate. We make our choice, but we do so out of a situation in which we are predisposed toward sin, and the predisposition comes from Adam's sin.

Carl Henry tackles this problem of our being bound by a decision and act of one whom we did not choose to be our representative. He notes that parallel cases occur in other areas, also. In children's court, for example, the court frequently names a guardian on behalf of an orphan. The child then is bound by the actions of a representative not of his own choosing.[9]

Finally, what about the effect of sin? The primary objective result of sin is separation from God.[10] Because God is a holy Being, the separation of man from Him is compounded by sin. God cannot permit any unholy thing in His presence. Sin is a veritable abomination to Him. There is therefore no basis on which forgiveness can be expected from Him as something deserved. Furthermore, sin has an incapacitating effect. What friction is to mechanical efficiency, sin is to spiritual efficiency. Sin hinders man's desire and effort to do good. As Paul put it, "For the good that I would I do not; but the evil which I would not, that I do" (Romans 7:19, KJV).

This, then, is man: an amazing combination of opposites. He was made in the image of God, or spiritually like God. Remnants of the image of God remain, and still glimmer through. Sin, however, came into the human race, through the sin of the first pair, Adam and Eve. All men now begin life out of proper fellowship with God, and consequently they sin, too. Unable to change themselves and to please God, all stand unrighteous in His sight.

CHRIST AND ATONEMENT

One's view of Jesus Christ brings him to the very center of his faith, since Jesus is the Founder and supreme Object of the faith of the Christian believer. The new evangelicals have maintained that it is here that the real test of one's theology and one's commitment takes place. Ramm says in an article entitled, "Jesus Christ, Hallmark of Orthodoxy":

> The basic text for purity of theological metal is whether there is devotion to his wonderful Person, loyalty to the apostolic doctrines summed up by his name, spiritual and heartfelt desire to "follow his steps" (I Pet. 2:21), and constancy "in the doctrine of Christ" (II John 9).[11]

This is not to say that other doctrines are unimportant to the new evangelicals. Rather it is to say that they regard this as the supreme and primary object of faith.

The orthodox view of the Person of Christ was given definitive formulation by the Council of Chalcedon (A.D. 451). This statement maintained several important tenets: that Jesus Christ was genuinely God, as fully so as the Father; that He was completely man, just as we are; that the humanity and deity were genuinely united in one person, rather than in some sort of split personality; and that the distinctive characteristics of humanity and deity were maintained, rather than being blended into some intermediate nature or hybrid form.

This formulation has come under criticism and reconstruction at various times in the history of the church. In particular, the liberalism of the later nineteenth and early twentieth century tended to modify the full deity of Jesus Christ. The story is told of W. Robertson Smith, the Scotch theologian, being accused of denying the divinity of Christ. Deeply hurt, he complained, "How can they say that? I've never denied the divinity of anyone!" Frequently the divinity of Christ in liberalism was one of difference of degree, rather than kind, from other men. All men have a spark of the divine in them; Jesus simply had more. Sometimes this came in the form of adoptionism: the view that because of His goodness, or receptiveness to God's working, Jesus was adopted as the Son of God.

Fundamentalism stood firmly upon the full deity of Jesus. An article on the deity of Christ was always included in the fundamentals, or was definitely implied by such items in the list as the virgin birth, the bodily resurrection, and the miracles. In so doing, however, there was a tendency to neglect the equally important fact of Jesus' full humanity. This is not surprising. Fundamentalism was a movement involved with defense, and one does not defend that which is not under attack. The humanity of Jesus was not being contested, since scarcely any liberal denied His humanity. The lack of positive presentation of this facet, however, was unfortunate. While it was certainly not a conscious departure from the orthodox theology, it did produce an over-emphasis which resulted in a practical neglect.

The new evangelicals are insistent that both dimensions of the Biblical teaching must be maintained. Real *incarnation* —that the second Person of the trinity, without ceasing to be fully God, also became fully man—must be insisted upon. The problem is that man is separated from God by the great gulf of sin. For fellowship between God and man to be reintroduced, the gap must be bridged. Someone who is both God and man must bring the two together. If Jesus was not fully God, the bridge does not quite meet at the divine end. If He was not completely man, the bridge does not reach to the human side. The full incarnation is not simply a theoretical problem of theology—it is a practical necessity upon which man's salvation rests.

The incarnation was accomplished through the virgin birth. During the fundamentalist-modernist controversy, the virgin birth was a point of considerable contention, in many cases becoming the virtual test by which orthodoxy of belief was believed to be discerned. While the new evangelicals see the continuing controversy over the virgin birth as unfortunate, they still feel that the doctrine must be maintained.

Carl Henry feels that one of the issues raised by the debate was the implied dismissal of the Biblical testimony. While the amount of Biblical evidence for the virgin birth is small, it is real, and any denial of it involves an undermining of the whole principle of Biblical authority. Henry also agrees with a number of items in Karl Barth's discussion of the virgin birth, and particularly with the claim that there is a theological necessity for the doctrine. While the incarnation and the virgin birth are not identical, there is a close connection between the two.[12]

Henry feels especially that the exclusion of the male in the virgin birth makes clear that a divine intervention has taken place. God has done something that man could not do. Henry also sees a special significance in the fact that it is the male parent who is excluded. While there is a sense in which this is self-explanatory, since the female is by nature always present at generation, yet Henry notes that the male takes the initiative in the act which leads to conception. This signifies that the incarnation, rather than being man's reaching up to God, had to be God's coming down to man. Henry also tends to feel that had Christ had two human parents, He would have been so much one with man that He could not have been a sinless sin-bearer.

Edward Carnell takes quite a different approach, however.[13] Observing that the Bible says that Christ was born of a virgin, but without specifying why, Carnell notes some explanations which have been given, and which he regards as false explanations: that Christ's deity required it, that His incarnation required it, and that His sinlessness required it.

Rather, Carnell feels that the virgin birth was a sign or evidence of the deity. It had to be a secret sign, or the enemies of God would have sought to destroy Jesus; yet for thirty years it was the only proof that Mary and Joseph had of Christ's divinity.

Since the virgin birth was not an essential to Christ's divinity, nor His sinlessness, there is no reference to it in the preaching and writing of the apostles. They rest their case upon the truth of His deity and the events flowing from it, rather than the sign.

Having affirmed their belief in the deity and humanity of Christ, the evangelicals are still more concerned with His work. Why did He come to earth? This involves certain conceptions flowing from the nature of God and of sin.

God, as we saw, is perfectly holy. His will is the standard of what is right and wrong. That which in any way does not accord perfectly with His will is sin. Man is a sinner; he falls short of the standard of perfection which is God. He cannot stop sinning, for his nature is distorted, or corrupted, in that direction. Even if he could, he would have no way of recompensing God for past sin. God, being a perfectly righteous Being, cannot tolerate sin in His presence, nor accept man without some payment being made and some covering being introduced to dispose of sin. Carnell says that God cannot forgive until the right moral conditions prevail. Christ has fulfilled these conditions.[14]

Christ came to atone for the sins of man. He had the intention and the function of introducing holiness into the human race, and of making man such that God could have fellowship with him once again.

How did Christ do that? He lived a perfect life, thus exemplifying what man should have been. He fully obeyed the will of God, although He could very well have sinned, since His temptation was genuine. Furthermore, He offered to God His life as a living sacrifice on the cross, more than the law required of Him. On the basis of His active and passive obedience, God is now able to forgive man.[15]

According to the "penal substitutionary" view of the atonement, Christ took the place of man and fulfilled what man should have done, namely to live a perfectly holy life. Moreover He bore the consequences of sin, which are death and at least temporary separation from the presence of God. Strictly speaking, it was not the exact consequences of sin, but rather an act or deed which God could consider equivalent. Thus, on the basis of what Christ offered to God, God can forgive man.

SALVATION

Justification means that God declares the sinner to be righteous, or just, in His sight. Spiritually, the believer is united with Jesus Christ so that his sin and guilt are transferred to Christ, and Christ's righteousness is considered to be his. This is a change of the status, or relationship, of the person to God, rather than an infusing, or actually making man good.[16]

The situation is somewhat parallel to a marriage. Suppose that a woman is deeply in debt and unable to raise funds to pay off her indebtedness. Then she marries an extremely wealthy man, whose wealth becomes hers, and she easily pays off her liabilities. There is a merging of the assets and liabilities of each to become the financial standing of both together.

Sin is not ignored. It was necessary for the penalty to be paid, so God could not simply forget about it. Similarly, it does not allow any encouragement for the idea that "I'm saved, so I can now do as I please," because the doctrine of salvation involves several other factors.

God grants forgiveness to man only when conversion takes place. Conversion involves two elements, both of which are functions of the whole man. Repentance is a realization of one's sinful state and condition, a feeling of godly sorrow or genuine remorse for sin, and a determination to abandon sin. It is not merely feeling sorrow for sin because of certain undesirable consequences which have occurred. It is regretting one's acts and thoughts because they are an offense against a holy God. It is a desire to abandon sin, even if one did not get caught and have to suffer as a result of his sin.[17]

The other half of conversion is faith, an act of trust in the Person of Christ for salvation. This trust is based upon the belief in certain truths as being so. One must have certain intellectual conceptions about the object of his faith, or he does not ordinarily commit himself.[18]

At conversion, justification takes place. These ought not to be thought of as a temporal sequence. Rather, they occur simultaneously, as does another aspect of the salvation experience: new birth.

The evangelist of the movement, Billy Graham, has stressed strongly that "Ye must be born again," echoing the words of Jesus to Nicodemus. God does not simply declare the sinner to be righteous; He also makes a change in the nature of the person. While the individual is not so transformed that he is now perfectly good and holy, a new disposition, or direction, is given.

From the new evangelicals' strong view of sin, one might conclude that this theology would be rather pessimistic regarding man and the possibility of his doing good. Similarly, since justification is an objective occurrence, performed externally to the person, it might seem to condone a libertine attitude with respect to personal Christian ethics. Neither of these assessments is correct, however, for both fail to take into account the important concept of regeneration, or new birth.

The Bible pictures man prior to conversion as being in some sense "dead." A person who is under the influence of an anesthetic is insensitive to stimuli. He can be pricked with sharp objects, or the dentist can drill in his tooth without his feeling any pain. Similarly, sin is a spiritual anesthetic. Spirtual stimuli do not produce any reaction in the unsaved man. He does not care about spiritual considerations, at least not very greatly. A part of his makeup, that which discerns and responds to spiritual values, is nonfunctioning. He is something less than full man as God originally intended him to be.

Regeneration means that God brings a man to life on a new level, or in a dimension which he has not previously experienced. He now feels more keenly the appeal of God in his life. Instead of an inclination toward sin or evil, he now feels a desire to live according to the values and goals God sets before him. This change is not a matter of reformation, a case of man mustering his will power and changing himself. It is rather a supernatural work of the Holy Spirit.

The new impulse is but the beginning of a process. The Christian life is not simply something that once happened. It is a continued development—a progress, or growth, in positive holiness—referred to as sanctification.[19]

Again, the process is not the Christian remaking himself. Rather it is bringing the condition of the believer into agreement with the status. Having declared him to be just in His sight, God actually makes the believer more like Himself. The image of Jesus Christ is implanted in his character. The Christian utilizes certain means and practices to receive this character: worship, the Word, the sacraments, self-denial, and a general life of love.[20]

Roman Catholic theology has tended to merge the two factors of justification and sanctification into one. In keeping with traditional Protestant orthodoxy, the new evangelicals keep them separated. Carnell distinguishes as follows:

> Justification is declaratory; sanctification is constitutive. Justification takes place once; sanctification is a lifelong process. Justification is a change in the sinner's relation to God; sanctification is a change in the sinner himself. Justification is objective; sanctification is subjective. Justification is an act done for us; sanctification is an act done in us.[21]

One further issue is whether the Christian ever arrives at

a state of complete freedom from sin in this life. There are some, termed "perfectionists," who maintain that the sinful nature, or sinful tendency, in man is "eradicated," removed, so that the person no longer commits sin. Carnell radically opposes this interpretation. The law requires that a man love God with all his heart, and his neighbor as himself. Surely no one can conscientiously say that man fulfills this. Furthermore, sin is not restricted to conscious deeds, as the perfectionist seems to think—it includes thoughts and attitudes as well. Jesus indicated that not only the external deed of murder is sin, but also hatred of one's brother. On this basis it would appear that spiritual perfection is only obtained when this life is over and the individual enters the direct presence of God.[22]

The Christian life is a struggle. While the believer is fully righteous in God's sight, he nonetheless has both the "old nature" (the tendency to sin) and the "new nature" (the desire to live a life of holiness). The Christian is always dependent upon the grace of God for victory in this warfare.

THE CHURCH

The experience of salvation leads logically to the doctrine of the church, for Christians do not simply exist as isolated individuals. The new evangelicals have not written a great deal directly on the church. One of the major contributions is an article by Carnell.[23]

In the primary definition of the church, Carnell follows the Reformed tradition. The church is all redeemed persons at all times, or, as he puts it, all who share in the Abrahamic covenant, regardless of restrictions or circumstances. It did not begin with the New Testament, but with the promise of God to Abraham that he and his children would be the special people of God, and would receive His salvation and blessings. In the New Testament and post-New Testament period, this was broadened. Paul says in Galatians 3 that the heirs of Abraham are not those who have Abraham's blood, but rather those who share his faith. Carnell supports this identification by showing that the Greek word *ecclesia,* or "church," is used of the congregation of Israel in the Septuagint, or Greek version, of the Old Testament. The church is simply the people of God.

Since we first encounter the church in its outward or empirical form, we sometimes make the mistake of defining it that way. Rather, the church is a spiritual phenomenon, a divinely created fellowship of sinners who trust the same saviour. The church is defined by its inclusion of saved persons, rather than Christians being defined by their connection with the church. The church is an invisible body which only becomes visible as its members meet together for worship, fellowship, and service.

The church does come to concrete realization, however. In various localities, believers gather together to build up one another and to carry out the Lord's command. This they can do more effectively together than separately. Five men, each trying individually to lift a piano up one-fifth of a flight of stairs, are much less efficient than all five together carrying it all the way. Similarly, local churches can forward the work of the Kingdom of God better than scattered individuals. This is a second meaning of the church, indeed the more frequent reference in the New Testament: the church at Corinth, at Rome, at Thessalonica.

Ideally, the universal, or invisible, church and the local, or visible, church should coincide. There should be no Christian outside the local church. There should be no non-Christian within the local church. In practice, however, the ideal is never realized. While every effort is made to ensure that only regenerate persons enter the membership of the church, realistic examination of even Jesus' teachings reveals that there are bound to be weeds among the grain, and that these will not be removed until the final judgment.

Local manifestations of the body of Christ need organizational structure, with boards, committees, and officers. It is a matter of expediency, a practical necessity for keeping the affairs of the church decent and orderly, and to facilitate the carrying out of the church's responsibility under her Lord. Carnell does not believe that the Scripture spells out anything specific about the form of government of the church; we are given some general principles of polity, but not details.

The New Testament does indicate that there were different types of ministry. The ministry of serving (the deacons) was established to relieve the apostles of certain mundane tasks which hindered the performance of their major function: prayer and ministry of the Word. There is still a need today for a pastor to delegate some of the more menial tasks to laymen so that he can give himself more fully to evangelizing the lost and building up the believers.

The ministry of teaching and ruling was the function of the elders, an office which existed in the church from the very beginning. There were already elders in the Jewish synagogue at the time of Christ, and the New Testament congregation drew upon that existing organizational structure. Paul appointed elders in each place where he founded a church, thus making clear that the same polity was to prevail in the Gentile churches.

What should be the nature of the officers in today's churches? Carnell notes that the passage in Acts 20 uses the terms bishop or overseer, presbyter or elder, and pastor or shepherd interchangeably. Therefore, any distinction between these officers derives not from principle, but from expediency. Further, he would hold that the ministry of rule is free to develop according to the needs of the times. Divergent modes of government may emerge as a result of different cultural factors or situations of expediency.

The exact titles of the officers are not of crucial importance. One denomination may have a supervising official whom it calls a bishop, and another may have a similar officer who is called an executive secretary. The title does not matter—the determinative question is whether this promotes or forwards the fellowship. The organization is a servant of the fellowship. The primary function regarding the organizational structure of the church is to determine what the Bible teaches. Second is the practical issue of carrying out the work of the church.

THE LAST THINGS

Eschatology is literally the study of last things. Actually the title tends to prejudice the issues in favor of a certain type of interpretation. The subjects of eschatology are of two major dimensions: individual eschatology, or the future events relating to individual persons; and cosmic eschatology, or the nature of the Kingdom of God and the future occurrences which will bring history to a close and cause far-reaching changes in the race, and indeed in the entire universe. The topics may be given either futuristic (eschatological) or noneschatological interpretations.

As to individual eschatology, the new evangelicals hold with the orthodox tradition that a part or aspect of man survives death. The soul, whether of the believer or the unbeliever, lives on even after its separation from the body at death. This condition is comparatively incomplete, however.[24]

In connection with Jesus' return, there will be a resurrection of the bodies of both the righteous and the unrighteous (although not necessarily both groups simultaneously), and the soul will be reunited with a changed body. The exact nature of this body is difficult to determine from the Scripture. While it will have some identification with the body possessed in this life, there cannot be simply a possession of the same molecules. The difficulties of the rather physical view are seen most fully in the historical problem of "Who Ate Roger Williams?"

Roger Williams, founder of the Providence, Rhode Island, colony and father of the Baptist movement in America, was buried and an apple tree was planted near his grave. Later, when it became necessary to exhume his body, it was found that the roots of the tree had followed along his skeleton, presumably because of the rich organic material there. Some of the molecules had formed apples and had undoubtedly been eaten. Thus, the same molecules may very well have been part of several different human bodies at different times.

Speculative questions about whose molecules they will be in the resurrection are not unlike the Sadducees' question about whose the wife of seven husbands would be in the resurrection. The resurrection is not simply a bringing back to life of the same physical body. It is a body which is somehow different, a glorified body. Whereas the liberals had held to the immortality of the soul, rather than the resurrection, and neo-orthodoxy has rejected the immortality of the soul in favor of the resurrection of the body, the new evangelicals believe the Bible teaches both.

Following the resurrection, there will be a great judgment in which the righteous and the unrighteous are separated on the basis of the relationship to Christ. Christians will spend eternity in the fellowship of God. Unbelievers will be subjected to endless punishment. The judgment will be final: no second chances or opportunities of reversing earthly decisions will be allowed.

In the general features, there is no difference between this view and that of fundamentalism. In the specifics, there are considerable differences. Fundamentalism often tended to conceive of heaven and hell in rather physical terms: hell was an actual physical flame; heaven was a place with literal geographical dimensions and gold-paved streets. For new evangelicals, eschatology is less literal and more spiritual: hell involves a suffering occasioned by separation from the presence of God, a mental anguish rather than physical pain;

heaven's glories are merely symbolized by the precious metals and the jewels. Nor is heaven a purely geographical location; it is not a place in the sense that one could get there by traveling far enough in a sufficiently powerful rocket ship. It is in a totally different dimension, and the passage is ordinarily made only by death.[25]

In the future events concerning the whole race or the whole creation, a rather pivotal topic in the discussion is the Kingdom of God. What is meant by the expression? Is this, which seems to occupy such an important place in the teaching of Jesus, a future occurrence, or is it a present reality? The issue has been a rather sharp point of disagreement among theologians.

Nineteenth-century liberals for the most part thought of the Kingdom as a present reality, the reign of God within human history. They were progressively building the Kingdom of God here on earth. At the start of the twentieth century, a new periodical was founded and named *The Christian Century,* in the belief that this was the century in which the Kingdom of God would be fully realized. Theologians like Ritschl and Harnack espoused a "realized eschatology." Christianity is a spiritual religion with ethical ends, the rule of God in the hearts of men, which was being gradually extended.

Some conservative theologians also stressed this present dimension of the Kingdom. While conceiving of the manner in which God exercises His reign in the hearts of men quite differently than Ritschl would, James Orr nonetheless thought of the Kingdom as primarily a new principle in society: the rule of God in human hearts, established by

Christ and designed to transform human society in all its relations.

Other conservatives moved strongly in the opposite direction, and in general that reactionary movement characterized fundamentalism. The Kingdom was thought of as an earthly millennial reign, to be inaugurated by the bodily return of Christ. In some cases, it was regarded as not merely the major dimension, but rather the *only* meaning of the Kingdom.

In particular, dispensationalism stressed the purely futuristic idea. According to that view, Jesus at His first coming offered to the Jewish people an earthly Kingdom. The Messianic Son of David was to sit on David's throne and rule over the nation from Jerusalem. Because Israel rejected the offer, it was postponed until the second coming of Christ. Then the Kingdom will be established, with Christ being recognized and accepted as her Messiah by Israel, which will have been gathered from around the earth and returned to her covenant land of Palestine. It is a serious mistake to try to build the Kingdom upon the first coming of Christ.

Rather definite practical consequences flow from these two different conceptions. Those who believe that the Kingdom is now here, as a spreading rule of Christ in human hearts, are quite optimistic about the possibilities of betterment of society. Those who see the Kingdom as totally future tend to be rather pessimistic, and feel that evangelism is the only real hope, and that this is not likely to prove very efficacious, either. The question is not merely a trivial one, then, as to whether the Kingdom is already in our midst and to be brought in by human effort, or totally future and following only upon Christ's return.

Many theologians have sought to synthesize these two dimensions, to make the Kingdom both present and future, an approach which has been taken by the new evangelicals. George Ladd notes that many of Jesus' teachings referred to the Kingdom as a seed sown in the hearts of men, a pearl which men can now acquire. Nonetheless, He also spoke of it as future, as being particularly connected with the "day of the Lord." Every attempt to eliminate either one of these by reducing it to the other has failed.[26]

How can the Kingdom be both, however? Ladd finds the key to this in understanding the meaning of "Kingdom." The primary meaning he finds to be not "realm," or a group of people over whom Christ exercises His authority, but "reign," or authority itself. While it is not possible for a realm, or domain, to be both present and future, a reign can be, and actually is.[27]

When a person commits himself in faith to Jesus Christ, he comes under the Lordship of Christ. Because sanctification is not total and immediate, the reign is not complete in any individual in this life. Furthermore, only a fraction of the human race accepts and acknowledges Christ as Lord. When He comes again in person, His Kingdom will be established fully. Every knee shall bow and every tongue shall confess Him as Lord, according to Philippians 2:10-11. The forces of evil will be brought into subjection, and God's saving purpose will be fully realized.

Another issue is whether the "Kingdom of Heaven" was postponed. According to dispensationalism, the Kingdom of Heaven is to be distinguished from the Kingdom of God. The Kingdom of God is the overall rule of God, while the Kingdom of Heaven is its earthly manifestation. It was the

Kingdom of Heaven which John announced and which Jesus offered to the Jews: if they had accepted it, Jesus would have actually set up an earthly Davidic reign. Is this distinction valid? Ladd maintains that it is not. It is true that Matthew uses the term "kingdom of heaven" thirty-three times, compared with only four instances of "kingdom of God," while Mark, Luke, and John uniformly use "kingdom of God" throughout.

Ladd notes, however, that in parallel passages Matthew uses "kingdom of heaven" where Mark or Luke use "kingdom of God." He concludes that these terms are interchangeable.[28] But why the different usage? Matthew was written primarily for Jews. But Jews regarded the primary name of their God (Jehovah) as so sacred that they did not even pronounce it. One of the ways of avoiding this difficulty was by substituting another word for God, and one of the most frequently used substitutes was "heaven" (literally, "the heavens"). Hence, "kingdom of heaven" would be simply a Jewish substitute for "kingdom of God." [29] For this and several other reasons, Ladd feels that the argument of a postponed earthly Kingdom simply cannot be sustained by the evidence.

While neo-evangelicalism has rejected the dispensational form of premillennialism, most of these men subscribe to a different form of premillennialism which goes back further in the history of the church. Premillennialism is simply the view that Christ will return personally and will then set up a reign on earth for a thousand years. Maintaining that the New Testament must be allowed to interpret the Old, rather than vice versa, Ladd examines the crucial passage in Revelation 20:1-6, which speaks of a first resurrection of certain righteous ones who lived and reigned for a period of a thousand years. The rest of the dead did not come to life until the end of the thousand years.

Amillennialists hold that there will not be any one-thousand-year earthly reign of Christ. They have ordinarily interpreted this passage by saying that the first resurrection is spiritual and the second is literal. The first refers to the new birth, the second to the resurrection of the body. The number "one thousand" is a symbol of the completeness of Christ's reign in the heart of the believer. Yet Ladd notes that the two references to "lived" (*ezesan*) are identical in form. There is no basis in the context for distinguishing the two, and therefore both resurrections ought to be interpreted in the same way. To do otherwise would be to abandon sound principles of hermeneutics (the science of interpretation) in favor of a meaning imported from outside the passage.[30]

The Bible speaks of a period of great tribulation which is to come at the end time (Matthew 24:21-28). Premillennialists are divided as to whether the church will be present during that period. Pretribulationists believe that Jesus' second coming will be in two stages, or phases: a "coming for" the saints at the beginning of the great tribulation, and a "coming with" them at the end of the tribulation (and the beginning of the millennium). The church, having been "raptured," escapes the great tribulation. References to the "elect" during the tribulation mean elect Jews, not the church. All dispensationalists are pretribulationists, although the converse is not necessarily true. Posttribulationists hold that there will be one unified return of Christ, and that it will come at the close of the tribulation. The church, being present, will have to endure the tribulation.

The new evangelicals seem rather uniformly to reject the pretribulational view which increasingly characterized fundamentalism. While the argument is quite lengthy and involved, it can perhaps be summarized by two contentions of Ladd's. First, any effort to separate the return of Christ into two phases by distinguishing among such terms as *parousia* (coming), *apokalypsis* (revelation), and *epiphaneia* (manifestation) cannot be sustained exegetically.[31] Second, the term "meet" in references to the church being caught up to meet the Lord is one which refers elsewhere to welcoming parties going out to meet a visitor, and then returning with Him.[32] For these and other reasons, the new evangelicals hold that the church will go through the tribulation.

IV

The Apologetic Orientation

A question of great importance to the new evangelicals is, "Is it true?" Having developed a system of theology, they are concerned to ascertain whether its beliefs correspond to reality, or are only the products of a fruitful imagination. To understand why this is so crucial, we must look at their view of faith and of its place.[1]

THE NATURE OF FAITH

Faith is basically trust or commitment, the giving of oneself to another. In this, the new evangelicals agree with the neo-orthodox that faith is no mere creedal assent; it is a personal relationship and involvement. But this dimension of trust, or, as Carnell terms it, "vital faith," is not to be divorced from another factor: belief, or "general faith." General faith is believing something to be so.

Vital faith, or personal trust, requires general faith. In ordinary life, this is true on several levels. A man does not embrace his wife without being certain that it is indeed his wife, and not a stranger. This may not be a very formal process ("Let's see: 5′ 6″, 120 lbs., brown hair, blue eyes. That's my wife, all right!"), but there is at least a preliminary reassuring glance. One does not hand his money to a person without ascertaining that it is his trusted friend, or an officer of the bank. The same is true in the relationship to God. One would not want to trust himself, his whole life, and even eternity, to what he thinks is God, without having some basis for believing that it really *is* God, not a projection of his father image, or something of that sort.

What is the relation of this faith to the proof or reasons that can be offered—or reason, as it is termed? Among the various answers that have been given, that of the new evangelicals needs to be seen in this context.

One approach has stressed the priority of reason over faith. Logically prior to, or independent of, any commitment to God or acceptance of revelation, one can prove the existence of God. This is believed to be based on the kind of evidence that would be accepted by any rational person. In this tradition, rational proofs such as those of Thomas Aquinas are offered. Some articles of faith, such as God's existence, can be proved. Others, such as the nature of God, must be taken upon authority, either that of the church or of the Bible. This view attempts to justify faith by making it as reasonable as any other belief.

The new evangelicals reject this viewpoint, on both philosophical and theological grounds. In their judgment, natural theology of this type cannot succeed, because it rests upon certain unproven assumptions. It is not a proof in an absolute sense. It is only a proof to those who would make those same assumptions. Furthermore, the arguments themselves are not fully valid. Whatever else they prove, they do not prove the Christian God. At best they may establish a limited being, perhaps even an impersonal being.

Why should the new evangelical be against the theistic proofs? Aren't they, after all, of some help in establishing certain features of the Biblical view? The answer given is that if they are invalid or unconvincing, the employment of them will in the long run undermine rather than support Christian faith. If one gives the impression that Christianity rests upon them, then their refutation may cause some persons to conclude that Christianity itself has been refuted. It is important, in other words, to put one's best foot forward.

The new evangelicals have also offered a theological explanation of their rejection of the natural theology approach, based upon the view of the sin of man. These theologians believe that when the first man, Adam, sinned, not only he but all of his descendents were affected in several ways. One was that sin damaged his powers of reason. Like mud obscuring clear water, sin obscures man's ability to recognize spiritual truth. Man can look at nature and conclude not that there is a personal creator-god, but that nature itself is a self-sufficient system. The effect of sin in blinding man to truth is greater the closer one gets to spiritual considerations. Sin has very little effect upon man's understanding of the technical formulae of chemistry. When it comes to man's understanding of God, however, sin is actually a state of rebellion against Him who is the object of the knowledge, and the confusion is greater.

Another concept of faith and reason is that which gives priority to faith. Sometimes called fideism, it maintains that belief must simply be based upon acceptance of authority, usually either that of the church or of the Bible. Reasons cannot be given. While fideism generally says that faith and its objects are above reason, variations of this position hold that faith is actually irrational, or anti-reason.

The new evangelicals are not warm toward this approach, either. In such an important matter as religion, how does one dare to believe in the absence of—or even the contradiction to—evidence? Suppose that one places his trust wrongly; he has lost or wasted his entire life. If a person investigates carefully and satisfies himself regarding an investment, certainly he ought to rest his choice of a life and world view upon an adequate basis. In particular, the new evangelicals have been quite critical of existential and neo-orthodox views that faith cannot be argued for, in the usual sense.

Having rejected these two rather common treatments of the relationship of faith and reason, the distinctive approach of the new evangelicalism becomes manifest. The basic thesis was propounded long ago by Augustine: faith must precede reason. Unless there is faith, reason cannot operate. It is not that I understand so that I may believe; rather, I believe so that I may understand. Faith is not the result or culmination of a process of reasoning; it is the very precondition of reasoning.

But what is this faith? Is it simply some blind or irrational commitment? Is it the sporadic choice of an object? Faith, as considered in this context, is for the new evangelicals as for Augustine a provisional acceptance of the world and life view revealed in Scripture. This means that while it cannot be proven antecedently to belief, once one has been willing to take the revelation at face value and consider the possibility that it is actually true and is the revealed Word of God, evidence may then be offered to that effect. Unless one is willing to make such an assumption, or, more technically such a presupposition, and then test it, he cannot see the rationality of the Christian world view.

The new evangelicals rather uniformly insist that there must be an unproven basic assumption, or presupposition: the existence of a God who has revealed Himself, particularly in the Scriptures. This thesis is stated in various forms by the several men, but is held in common by all of them. They would, in fact, insist that the existence of God is the necessary presupposition for affirming intelligibility anywhere. Ramm has given probably the most complete statement:

> We assert as our fundamental apologetic thesis the following: "there is an infinite, all-wise, all-powerful, all-loving God who has revealed Himself by means natural and supernatural in creation, in the nature of man, in the history of Israel and the Church, in the pages of Holy Scripture, in the incarnation of God in Christ, and in the heart of the believer by the gospel." [2]

Several observations should be made about the presuppositional approach. First, the basic assumption, or tenet, is supplied by the Scriptures, rather than being constructed by unaided human reason. It has not been derived from sense experience, and is therefore not natural theology in the sense given earlier.

Second, it is definitely an assumption. There is no claim that this principle or statement can be antecedently established by appealing to anything more basic, such as sense perception. This is an ultimate, or a starting point. While assumption may not be consciously made, it is nonetheless assumed. The new evangelicals will maintain that every system must have some unproven assumption with which it begins its reasoning.

One must begin with faith, then. Without reliance upon the knowledge of God as revealed in the Bible, at least by a tentative acceptance, one would never really come to know Him. Yet faith in the sense of a provisional acceptance of something not initially proved need not remain on this level. It can go on to be verified, or at least vindicated, so that the assumption is not irrational. Faith does not fly in the face of reason. Reason is here performing a different function from that which it fulfills in natural theology. While reason cannot discover the content of faith, it can show the reasonability of faith, once the initial provisional acceptance has been made of that which has been revealed.

At this point, it might appear that the presuppositionalist strategy has played directly into the hands of secular critics, who often make a distinction between knowledge and faith. Knowledge is the domain of reason; its objects are definite and have been proved; it deals with the material of science. Faith, on the other hand, is according to this view the acceptance of unproved statements. There is a qualitative difference between these two realms. The Christian has faith, which sometimes is believed to verge on superstition, while the scientist has knowledge.

The apologetic method of presuppositionalism is clear, however. It seeks to remove the neat dichotomy, not in the Thomistic fashion of denying the priority of faith, but by showing that there is really no such thing as "pure knowledge," if knowledge is conceived of as consisting of reason alone and containing no unproved assumptions. While one must begin any system with general faith, he can then go on to offer reasons for such an acceptance or commitment. Not only does the Christian believer have faith; so does everyone else.[3]

Most philosophies, for example, are empiricisms. They maintain that knowledge or truth is gained through the experience of the five senses. How does one establish this? If he questions that the sense experience is of objects which actually exist independently of his experience, and that the sense datum he has corresponds to the actual object, there really is no answer. If I look at an apple on a table and ask myself how I know that my visual experience is accurate, I can feel of the apple, thus employing a different sense. But how do I know that my tactile sense is accurate? In the final analysis, I either must say that it makes no difference whether there really is anything "out there" or whether my experience is true and accurate, or I must admit that I simply assume it; that is, I take it "on faith." At least, it certainly appears that the statement, "all knowledge comes from sense perception," cannot itself be verified by sense perception.

Most philosophers attempt to communicate their views to

others. If they do not seek to persuade others of their philosophical conceptions, at least they attempt to make known various ideas or wants, such as, "I would like the salt, please." In the process, there is the assumption that some sort of meaningful communication is possible. One proceeds on the basis of there being a common sphere of meaning and understanding, so that the other person recognizes what he means by the salt and can understand his desire. Yet how does one establish that there is such a universe of communication? He doesn't. He simply assumes it—and must, if he is to communicate. It is not a necessary assumption, unless one must communicate, but since one cannot get inside another's mind and know the other's thoughts, it cannot be "proved."

Instances could be multiplied. Science also must make certain assumptions. In epistemology (the theory of knowledge) it must be assumed that knowledge is possible. Certain ethical assumptions are made, such as that the scientist ought to be honest in his experimentation and reports, even if he could fudge on his data and get away with it. Metaphysical assumptions are also made, such as the regularity of the universe and its continuous functions. The new evangelicals maintain that every reason has its faith, in the sense of some assumption or set of assumptions which must initially be provisionally accepted.

The Christian theology, its view of God and the world and the relation between them, is seen not to be badly off, when all the considerations are examined. While it cannot be said that it can be proved, in the sense of starting from some firmly established or publicly demonstrable facts and arguing deductively, it would be the contention of the new evangelicals that *nothing* can really be "proved" in the strict sense. They will argue, however, that the system established by the basic Christian assumption can then be shown to give a better explanation of the whole of reality than does any other view.

But philosophers comprise only a very small proportion of the general population. What about the ordinary man in the street? Does all of this have any significance for him? Here the new evangelicals maintain what might be termed the "inevitability of philosophy." Every man must to some extent philosophize. They do not mean by this that all men are technically skilled abstract thinkers, but that all men of necessity form a view of the nature of things, the purpose of life, or where history is moving. This is necessary in order to act. As uncritical and crude as this view may be, it is nonetheless present. A person without any conception of the meaning and direction of the world and of life would find himself caught in uncertainty and insecurity. Indeed, modern man frequently finds himself in that situation, a condition which Carnell calls "soul-sickness."

The practical human predicament is a result of the discrepancy between the real and the ideal, and the effort to bring the two together. The fear of death contributes, also. This practical human predicament is paralleled by a theoretical human predicament. All about us we find facts: specific objects, particular events. What is the meaning of them? Can some explanation be given? What causes them to exist or to occur? What is the moving force behind history? Is there one concept, or system, that will bring all of the many phenomena together into a coherent unity? This is the philosophical problem of the one and the many.

The evangelical theologians say that, since man must have an understanding of the universe about him in order to live meaningfully, Christianity can be shown to be true if it can be demonstrated that it gives a more complete and consistent explanation of our universe than any other competitive system, and if it satisfies the need of the human heart.

What, then, are the bases upon which belief in Christianity (or, more correctly, belief in Jesus Christ) rests? Roughly, there are two major divisions of considerations— practical considerations, and theoretical, or rational, grounds.

PRAGMATIC EVIDENCE

Someone has said that the most important question to contemporary man is not "Is it true?" but rather "Is it relevant?" No matter how impressive the reasons offered for the truthfulness of a statement or system, man is not too likely to commit himself to it unless he sees its practical value. The heart of man has certain needs, and man is seeking for the satisfaction of these needs.

It is in Christianity that they are most fully met, claim the new evangelical theologians. Augustine said that the heart of man is restless, and does not find rest until it finds it in God. Similarly, these men hold that God is the satisfaction of the needs and desires of man.[4]

The spiritual needs of man are many. Peace of mind is sought, yet the goal is elusive because of man's feelings of guilt. As hard as he tries to live a good life and to suppress guilt feelings, his conscience still frequently condemns him. Even the man who seems to have no remorse over "evil" in his life cannot avoid moments of grave concern. Pathological guilt feelings aside, a certain amount of guilt awareness is appropriate, because man is actually a sinner, and therefore guilty in the sight of God. The feelings of guilt can only be removed when the objective fact of guilt is removed. The gospel of Jesus Christ announces that because of His death and resurrection, the man who believes becomes righteous in the sight of God.

Man also yearns for immortality. He has aspirations as to what he would like to achieve or accomplish, but these aspirations and hopes are not fully realized, because he is limited to the proverbial threescore years and ten. So much left to do, and so much to accomplish, to become, and such a shortness of time! Although medical science has prolonged life and delayed the grim day, death nevertheless comes to every man. The haunting question of whether there is anything beyond this life, and if so, whether he is prepared for it, disturbs many a man. In Christian faith this longing is also satisfied. The message of Christianity is that Christ has obtained victory over death, this being particularly signified by Jesus' resurrection. The believer looks upon death not as the termination of life, but rather as a transfer from one mode, or form, of life to another.

What view or set of values is really adequate as an object of my commitment? This is a problem which concerns every man, and it is a question to which every man gives an answer by his life, whether he really reflects upon it or not. In his *Philosophy of the Christian Religion* Carnell examines a series of alternatives.[5] A wise choice of life-view is one which will not disappoint when carried out to its full implications.

Typical of Carnell's argumentation is his treatment of the first rather obvious option, immediate pleasure. While this brings satisfaction for a time, eventually the person grows bored, and turns elsewhere for satisfaction. Immediate pleasure has failed, for its value is not lasting.[6] Examining other options, such as communism, humanism, Roman Catholicism, and Kierkegaardian existentialism, Carnell concludes that the heart can only be satisfied by Biblical Christianity. Verification at this level can in part be done through observation of the consequences. In the fullest sense, however, verification is possible only for the person who has personally participated.

A few years ago an unbelieving scholar toured Australia holding public meetings in which he challenged the truthfulness of Christianity, exposing what he felt were its weaknesses. Each night he would ask, "Are there any questions?" One night an old farmer emerged from the crowd and came to the platform, peeling an orange as he came. He then proceeded to eat the orange before the flabbergasted speaker. Then he asked, "Was the orange which I just ate sweet or sour?"

The speaker replied, "How should I know? I didn't taste it."

"And neither have you tasted Christianity," retorted the farmer. "I have, and I've found it to be true."

The first basis for accepting Christianity as true is that it meets the needs of the human heart. It brings satisfaction for its longings, quiet to the gnawings of a guilty conscience, hope for the future. This variety of apologetic argumentation has certain inherent shortcomings, however, since psychology can offer alternative explanations for these phenomena of experience, besides the truthfulness of the object of belief. Therefore, there must be theoretical considerations in addition to the practical.

The theoretical arguments are of two general types, logical and factual. Another way of speaking might be to refer to them as internal criteria and external criteria.

LOGICAL EVIDENCE

The internal, or logical, factor is simply the consistency of the system. The Christian religion has a set of fundamental theological propositions which form an interrelated noncontradictory system of religious truth. The evangelicals claim that this standard is used virtually universally as a test for truth (or negatively, as a means for detection of error). If a witness in a courtroom trial contradicts himself, he is generally considered to have told an untruth in one assertion or the other (or, indeed, possibly in both). Both the A statement and its contradiction cannot be true in a meaningful, rational world. This is known in logic as the Law of Contradiction, formulated by Aristotle: a thing cannot both be A and not-A at the same time and in the same respect. Unless one proceeds on this assumption, there can be no meaningful knowledge or communication, since anything could therefore be both true and false at the same time.[7]

The new evangelicals have not carried the analysis of

Christianity under this criterion very far. One might wish that this analysis had been applied in additional areas, although it is of course more of a defensive reply to specific charges. These men recognize that the knowledge of theological truths is in some respects limited. We do not know all or understand completely—God is not fully comprehended, for instance. This ought not to cause consternation, unless one holds that what is not known exhaustively is not really genuine knowledge, or is therefore not possible.

Carnell tells of the centipede who had no difficulty walking until someone asked him to explain how he did it. When he thought of all his legs, the complexity of movement involved, and the difficulty of coordination, he was overwhelmed with a sense of the impossibility of walking and became immobile. Similarly, there are many things we do not understand about God. However, we can at least see the direction from which resolution would probably come if we had more information.

An example is the doctrine of the trinity. On the face of it, this seems to be a formal contradiction, since it asserts that God is one and that God is three. Yet the Law of Contradiction says, ". . . in the same respect," and the suggestion here is that God is one in a different respect than He is three. What these two different respects are and how they are related to one another is not yet completely clear. We are faced with a mystery, but at least it is not an internal contradiction.

There is, in the Christian system, a unity. The major themes or doctrines fit together harmoniously. The various books of the Bible display a remarkable oneness. Although

there is a progressive development from the less complex
to the more detailed, there is nonetheless a singularity of
message.

Consistency also means that a world-view fulfills the criteria which it sets for itself. Here is a fundamental point of
evaluation, or criticism. A system may be criticized on one
of two grounds: the degree to which it fulfills the criteria
which it particularly espouses, or the degree to which it
fulfills the criteria which all world-views must meet. It cannot legitimately be criticized by another philosophy for failing to meet the criteria accepted by the latter but not by the
former.

This means, for instance, that Christianity may not be
criticized on the grounds that it does not provide the maximum pleasure for the maximum number of persons within
the earthly life. It does not make man the highest value. It
puts God at the center and makes His glory the highest
value. Further, this life is not all that there is. To criticize
Christianity on the above criteria, as a humanist would perhaps do, is invalid unless it can be established that pleasure
is a principle which all world-views must satisfy. Similarly,
it is no damage to Buddhism that it does not particularly
integrate with specifics of history, for Buddhism is not dependent upon historical events. Christianity must fit the
facts of history, though, since it claims to be dependent
upon certain concrete events, such as the life, death, and
resurrection of Jesus Christ and the dealings of God with
the nation of Israel.

An analogy drawn from the athletic realm may help to
explain this point. Different football teams have different

strategies. Some concentrate on defense, having as their major aim the prevention of opposition scoring. Others endeavor to score heavily, favoring offense. If a defense-minded team scores only one touchdown, it really cannot be sharply criticized, for it has not really espoused the value of large scores. If it has held the opposition scoreless, it has played a "good game"; it has fulfilled its objective. If the opposition has scored heavily, the team has played a poor game; it has failed to accomplish its aim. If, however, it holds the opposition to a single field goal (a rather good defensive performance), but has failed to score at all, its performance is deemed inadequate, since it has failed to meet the criterion which presumably all football teams espouse, namely, ending the game with more points than the opposition.

Christianity must fulfill the criteria which it has set for itself. It maintains that man has been made for fellowship with God and that this is established through faith in Jesus Christ. Then it is that the deepest needs and yearnings of the human heart are satisfied. It claims to relate to history, and can be shown to be tangent with historical fact. Christianity can be said to be internally consistent, therefore, in two respects: it contains no contradictions within its tenets, and it fulfills the objectives which it sets for itself.

Is such logical or formal criterion enough? It is possible to construct a system entirely free from internal contradictions and yet unrelated to reality. The presence of contradiction simply indicates that untruth or error are present. The absence of contradiction does not establish the presence of truth. One could even imagine such a system that is internally consistent and satisfying to man, and still empty of truth. Indeed, another might bring greater pleasure if it offered all that Christianity does, but without the corresponding demands. Mere existential relevance and logical consistency are not enough by themselves. Christianity can only be considered to be true if it corresponds to external data.

Christianity is true, and in three different areas. It is factually true: the historical events claimed to be involved in the Christian religion can be seen to have occurred, at least so far as data is available for checking. It is supernaturally true: there are evidences which indicate that forces were at work which were of more than merely human origin. Finally, it is metaphysically true: it gives a better explanation of the whole phenomena of our experience and of the universe than any alternative view.

HISTORICAL EVIDENCE

The Christian religion can be seen to mesh with reality in several different areas.[8] There is first the geography of the Bible: the numerous references to rivers, mountains, lakes, and plains. Some of the references are such that we do not fully understand what is designated, or we do not now have complete geographical information, but it is not necessary to be able to confirm every reference. In those cases where we have adequate data to assess the accuracy of the statements, there is a high degree of correlation with known information.

There are numerous references to culture, both material

and social. Such matters as birth rites, legal systems, and
burial rites are frequently mentioned. Here again, the references are appropriate to the practices of the time.

The Bible also makes many historical references as to
kings and military campaigns. Not every historical detail of
the Bible has been confirmed, nor is each likely ever to
be. In some cases, the requisite information may have been
lost to us. The record is not completely free of difficulties,
but the trend of archaeology has been strongly in the direction of confirming the Bible's historical accuracy.

One hundred years ago it was fairly widely held that the
Bible was full of errors. The reference to Sargon (Isaiah
20:1) was considered one of these. Similarly, Daniel indicated that Belshazzar was the last king of Babylon, whereas
the Babylonian records seemed to name Nabonidus as the
last king. Records have been discovered, however, establishing a co-regency of Belshazzar and Nabonidus, thus confirming the accuracy of the Biblical record.

Finally, the Bible's references to nature are accurate.
This topic falls into the area of Bible and science, which is
such a major discipline as to deserve separate treatment.
Nonetheless, it appears that the scientific references of the
Bible, properly interpreted, are in harmony with the data of
science when properly understood.

Of what difference is the Bible's factual accuracy? To be
sure, it is quite possible for the Bible to be accurate and not
be of divine origin. If, however, the Bible is true in its
references, then no objection can be made to its claimed
inspiration on the basis that errors are present. If the Bible
has been given by a God who knows all and is capable of

communicating truth, then one would expect that the Bible should be correct in its references. This it is shown to be.

There are some propositions in the Bible which do not admit of factual verification. The theological propositions in the Bible are not ordinarily considered to be empirically verifiable. That the Bible is correct in the references that can be checked does not establish the truthfulness of its theological propositions, but if the former proved to be false, on what basis would one continue to hold the latter? Would not the propositions be rendered suspect? If we discover that a person is lying or mistaken in areas where we can check his word, does this not also undermine our confidence in his testimony in general? On the other hand, correctness in testable areas does lend a certain presumption of truthfulness in other areas as well.

SUPERNATURAL EVIDENCE

Still another element is needed. A religion could have historical basis, and its record be accurate, without necessarily being either of divine origin or true. What about Christianity? Can it be explained adequately in natural categories, or is there anything about it which bears the trademark of the supernatural? There is the claim of miracles, fulfilled prophecy, and the supernatural Person of Christ, particularly His bodily resurrection. Because prophecy has been examined earlier, miracles will receive the major treatment here.

Before miracles can be discussed, they must be defined. Ramm suggests three qualities of a miracle: it is a sensible event, it is such as to suggest strongly and clearly the presence of the supernatural, and it is done within a redemptive context.[9] Such supernatural acts of God as the regeneration of the human soul are not, strictly speaking, to be classed as miracles.

But what of the relation of miracle to natural law? David Hume had defined a miracle as a violation of natural law. Consequently a prejudice against miracles was immediately introduced, since this suggested that miracles are violent and disruptive. Two different views appear to be held among the new evangelicals. Carnell suggests in his *Apologetics* that miracles are based upon a type of law with which we are not familiar, but which is nonetheless a law.[10] He is broadening somewhat the usual meaning of law. If we had sufficient knowledge, we could understand why and when a miracle occurs, and could perhaps even predict its occurrence. Ramm, however, regards miracles as acts of creation, maintaining that it is meaningless to speak of miracles as functionings of law, since this is contrary to the usual meaning of law and really could only be considered to be laws from God's standpoint (if, by this, it is meant that in a given situation God would always do the same thing).[11]

The real issue in discussing the possibility of miracles is the underlying world-view. It is not sufficient simply to argue the historical evidence regarding miracles, since the view of reality held by the historian determines to a large extent what he will accept as evidence. Rather than admitting any real evidence of the supernatural, a naturalist would probably explain such apparent data on another basis. Thus, both Ramm and Carnell insist that Christian miracles can only be properly evaluated within the context of the Christian system. Within this framework their rationality is not only plausible, it is forceful.

What is called for, then, is an openness of approach to the matter. Instead of coming to the discussion with either a preconception that miracles have occurred or that they cannot, one ought to be open to the possibility that they may or may not have occurred, and willing to accept tentatively or provisionally either of the two alternatives.

Experience alone cannot sustain the idea that there cannot be miracles. On the basis of pure empiricism, anything and its opposite are equally possible. Only if one has a preconception of the nature of reality can he say that miracles cannot occur. Such a world-view must itself be substantiated, and the new evangelicals engage in thorough rebuttals of naturalism.

With the presupposition of the possibility of a theistic world-view, the evidence for the miracles is strong. Ramm points out that Jesus Himself appealed to His miracles as proof of His deity, and there is a wonderful correspondence between His words and His miraculous deeds. The gospel accounts become meaningless if the miracle records are removed from them. Furthermore, despite the objections of David Hume, the testimony to the miracles is adequate and sufficient. They are to be accepted as historically real. There was a great variety of miracles and they occurred over a period of time. Many of them were performed in public, and some were performed in the company of unbelievers and even of enemies. This last point is of considerable importance, for there were individuals who would have delighted to expose Christ's miracles as fraudulent, yet none apparently attempted to do so.

Alternative explanations can be offered for the miracles, of course. The simplest and most plausible explanation, however, according to the new evangelicals, is that a super natural Divine Being produced effects which men could not have done. There is evidence that Christianity is of supernatural origin, and therefore true.

METAPHYSICAL EVIDENCE

Finally, the Christian world-view gives metaphysical intelligibility to the universe. When we look at the phenomena of man, history, ethics, aesthetics, and epistemology, the Christian view gives a more adequate explanation than does any other competitive system. It makes sense of the vast variety of data.[12]

There are a number of areas in which this metaphysical intelligibility is seen, one being the theory of knowledge, or epistemology. Carnell observes that there seems to be a certain structure of the intellect, common to all men, which makes knowledge possible. In particular, all men seem to operate with the Law of Contradiction already mentioned. This is requisite to knowledge in several respects.[13]

The Law of Contradiction is essential to sense perception. The telephone pole which I now observe cannot at the same time and in the same respect be the grass, which I am also observing. If it is possible for something to be both A and not-A, I cannot have sense perception. Everything would be confused into one great blur, or the "bloomin', buzzin' confusion" that William James spoke of. It is also essential to truth, or speech.

This principle must be innate, or built into the very structure of man's mind. Man cannot begin life with his mind a blank tablet. In the empirical view, the Law of Contradiction would be learned from sense experience, but, Carnell argues, how could there even be that first experience unless man came to it already possessing the Law of Contradiction and perhaps others as well?

Immanuel Kant had worked out an elaborate system of categories of the understanding, involving some twelve in all, which enable men to order the raw material of experience into knowledge. Yet Kant never really asked or answered the question of how it is that all men possess these categories. Carnell answers the question by saying that the Christian view gives a more satisfactory answer than any other that has been offered. The Bible says that God made man in His own image; and God, being a reasonable Being, presumably included the power of reason represented by the categories. Thus, the new evangelicals would hold an epistemology which Ramm calls "authoritarian rationalism." [14]

Carnell appeals also to the area of ethics. He notes that we proceed on the basis that there is a difference between right and wrong, although men may disagree, and quite radically so, on what is right and what is wrong. There also seems to be a compulsion to do what is right and not wrong. This is called conscience, and all men have it.

Meaningful moral judgments presuppose some objective standard of ethics.[15] Some have maintained that this does not require knowledge of an absolute standard (as that this is right, period, because God has declared that this is right). It is only necessary to be able to note comparative quality of judgments (as that this is better than that course of action).[16] Sometimes the analogy of length is used. In order to determine which of two sticks is longer, it is not necessary to have a yardstick (an absolute measure of length) to measure them and then compare the figures. One need only lay one stick alongside the other to see which is longer. The answer is not subjective, that is, one person's own judgment of length, and all men would agree that one is longer. So, the argument says, are moral actions. We do not need some absolute measure of the goodness of an action or a judgment to be able to decide its worth. We only need to compare it with other contemplated courses of action, and choose the best.

The analogy breaks down, however, if Carnell's reasoning is correct. It is not as simple as saying, "We can see which stick is longer." The question is, Where do we get the concept of length? How did we come to be able to recognize length as contrasted with color or fixity of position? While this may not seem to be too crucial to the issue of length (conceding, as it were, the empiricist position), what of goodness or rightness? How do we recognize them? Although we may not be able to tell *how* good an action is, if we are even to talk meaningfully about the difference between good and bad, or one instance being better than another, there must already be a standard of rightness or of goodness within the person.

The objector may well interrupt to assert again that no absolute is needed. We simply hold certain things to be right or good because the particular society of which we are a part has taught us so. But that misses the point. Apart from the question of how the first persons decided on the good and the right and started the process, the issue really is, Why ought one to do what his society has decided is right or wrong? or, Why ought one to pursue the values he has espoused?

An illustration or two may make the point clearer. In our society, scholars have a certain code of ethics. They are to report their findings honestly. They are not to produce fraudulent data in order to establish their hypotheses, even if they can escape detection. This, it would be maintained by many, is not because there is something inherently wrong in dishonesty, but because the scholar had bound himself by certain canons of his profession. But why ought he to follow those canons if it would not be to his personal advantage to do so? Who says he ought to follow relative standards?

Or suppose a student comes to his professor in great distress. The student had done all "A" and "B" work in the course, and yet his grade report indicates an "F." Why, he asks the professor, has he received such a grade? The professor's answer is a bit shocking: "I don't like you, and that's how I treat students I dislike." Let's follow the conversation further.

STUDENT: "But that's not right of you. I deserved at least a 'B.' "

PROFESSOR: "Why do you say that's not right? Do you have some sort of absolute moral standard?"

STUDENT: "No, but you are a member of the academic community. You are bound to abide by the code of professorial ethics."

PROFESSOR: "I choose to follow that when it pleases me. It didn't in this case, and I have destroyed all the test papers, so there is no proof that I cheated you. I cannot be caught."

STUDENT: "But when you signed your contract, you in effect swore to abide by the code."

PROFESSOR: "I had my fingers crossed when I signed that."

STUDENT: "But it's not right. It just isn't."

PROFESSOR: "I'm sorry, but I'm terribly busy. Good day, young man."

The point of the discussion is this: a relative ethic reduces down to subjectivism unless there is some truly objective point. Although a given action is right or wrong, depending upon the circumstances, we usually say that in a set of circumstances there is a difference between right and wrong which goes beyond mere personal pleasure or displeasure. Although the content of *what* is right may well be relative (for the sake of this argument), the sense that one *ought* to do the right is not. What authority is there for such a statement? Carnell and the other new evangelicals would say that there is a Supreme Being, infinite in wisdom, power, and goodness, and that He who made all things and all persons is the Originator, Guarantor, and Supporter of moral values. I ought to because He says so, and I feel this compulsion because, once again, He has made me in His own (moral) image.

Further, all nations and tribes on the earth have moral laws, although the content of these laws is greatly varied. Even criminals have standards of ethics, as distorted as they

may seem to more law-abiding citizens. Whenever a man
tries to insist that either he or another ought to do or believe
something, he is starting upon a series of questions which
ends with an ultimate "Why?" which can be best satisfied by
the Biblical answer: "God." Because many men do not
carry through consistently on their questioning, or because
they do not consider the nature of the Biblical answer, they
do not come to the Christian conclusion.

In a later book, *Christian Commitment,* Carnell argues
the ethical issue from another standpoint.[17] Here he appeals to what he calls the "judicial sentiment." When we
feel that someone has infringed upon our rights, we judge
him guilty; he ought to be punished for it. Yet we do not
generally see ourselves as the proper enforcers of this moral
right. It is necessary to introduce the Supreme Being, God,
as the Judge. This differs from the argument of Immanuel
Kant in his *Critique of Practical Reason,* in that Kant introduced God as the Guarantor of one's own moral values,
or as the conscience which accuses oneself, whereas this
judicial sentiment accuses the other. Kant's argument is
similar to Carnell's first argument.

In short, then, Carnell would argue that the way in which
men live presupposes some objective moral standard. He
would further maintain that the Christian view of God and
the world explains this better than any other world-view. In
addition, he would extend the same sort of argument to
esthetic judgments, claiming that they also require objective
standards, and that once again the best explanation is God
and His working.

The new evangelicals scrutinize not only man's moral

and spiritual environment, but also his physical environment. Here men conduct themselves in such a way as to imply a certain view of reality. The Christian world-view offers the best justification.

Probably the leading example is the so-called uniformity of nature. All sane men ordinarily proceed on the assumption that the future will be like the past. Thus, one assumes that the sun will rise tomorrow as it has in the past. He assumes that at sea-level, all other factors being equal, water will boil at 212 degrees Fahrenheit tomorrow as it did yesterday. How does one justify this, however? As Carnell points out, there is no empirical proof.[18] At best it is a deduction from other concepts, as that there is some force at work preserving the world and its operations and guaranteeing this uniformity. Henry correctly observes that the confidence in the continuance of the universe arose from a theistic interpretation of the universe, in which God was seen as both making and preserving all things. One must have some explanatory basis for the orderliness and continuity of nature and life. The best basis is theism.

There is also a remarkable order in the physical universe, almost as if it were adapted to man's needs. While Darwinism offered an alternative explanation of the apparent design in the organic elements of the universe, it could not similarly account for the inorganic order. Indeed, the new evangelical apologists would maintain that the fact of order even in the organic universe can also be *better* explained by the Christian theistic hypothesis than by the proposition that chance factors and natural selection accomplished it.

Although the argument is carried into other areas, the general development can perhaps be summarized at this point. The new evangelicals call attention to certain features of the moral, intellectual, and physical universe, and claim that the Christian theistic world-view presented in the Scripture gives a more adequate explanation than any alternative view.

Among these phenomena are the need of objective standards of ethics, truth, perception, and esthetics; the uniformity of the universe; the fact of order in the universe. A person possessed of an inquiring mind is driven to ask the question, "How did the universe get to be this way?" One can answer with any of several naturalistic philosophies: "It just happened. Chance factors have made it this way. Built into the nature of the universe are certain moral values." Or he can take the approach of Biblical revelation which says: "There is an all-powerful, all-wise, all-loving God who has made and who sustains all that is." The new evangelicals would claim that their view of the world and life does a more adequate job of explaining all of the data. It does this with fewer assumptions, with less distortion, and by eliminating fewer relevant considerations than does any competitive view.

To be sure, one's antecedent view of possibility will go a long way to determine which alternative is to be accepted. If one comes to the issue with the conviction that there is no supernatural power and no purpose in the universe, then theism must be rejected. The new evangelicals would contend that if a person is really willing to re-examine such a belief and consider the Christian theistic assumption, there is adequate evidence for the greater plausibility of the latter.

Is this not simply another instance of natural theology? The definition given earlier is of importance here. Natural theology makes no appeal to the Biblical revelation, whereas this approach proceeds with the hypothesis of God and His relationship to the creation, as spelled out in the Bible. The situation is like having the right answer to a riddle, and then checking it out against the question contained in the riddle, to see how well it satisfies the requirements. Another analogy would be checking a given answer to a mathematical problem and seeing that it fits the demands of the problem. Whereas it might have been quite difficult to deduce the answer from the riddle or the solution from the mathematical problem itself, it is easier to recognize the true answer when it has been supplied in advance.

These men would therefore claim that it is only when one's view of God has the richness of detail supplied by the Biblical account that one can recognize Him in nature, and that these details of the nature of God and His relation to the universe are not extracted from a mere observation of the phenomena themselves. That some create a natural theology which is persuasive to themselves is not overly impressive to these apologists. One must rather ask, they would say, whether the natural theologian is really that, or if he, like Thomas Aquinas, has benefited from knowledge of the content of the Biblical revelation and commitment to the Creator.

Natural Science and Biblical Theology

The relationship of Bible and theology to natural science is of such major proportions as to require an extensive separate treatment. Certain issues have been touched on in the doctrine of man. Here we will simply note the new evangelicals' view of the relationship between theology and science.

Friction has sometimes arisen between these two disciplines because practioners in one or the other (or both) failed to understand the distinctive role and function of each. Science is concerned with the structure and causal, or functional, relationships of the *physical* and *space-time* aspects of the universe. It deals with the *how* of nature's processes. Theology, on the other hand, is primarily the study of God and of His relations to the created universe, including man. Insofar as it deals with matters of nature, it answers the question of *why*.

There is consequently no conflict between the Bible's saying that God created the earth (Genesis 1:1), and the theory that the earth began when a passing heavenly body pulled a molten portion from the sun which cooled and formed our earth. The Bible does not tell us how God did it; it merely tells us that He did it and why He did it. As I sit in the dentist's chair pondering the hole in my tooth, there is no inconsistency between saying that the drill made it and that the dentist made it. The hole is there because the whirling bit of the drill ground off a portion of the tooth. It is also there because the dentist intelligently and purposefully applied the drill so that he could remove the decay and fill the tooth, restoring it to soundness and health. Both are legitimate explanations, but explanations of different sorts.

Conflict between science and theology may arise for several reasons, but ideally the two should exist in a state of harmony. In areas where the Bible has implications of a scientific character, an effort should be made to discover and demonstrate the grounds of this harmony.[19]

The age of the earth has presented considerable difficulty. Whereas many believed the Bible taught that the earth had been created in six literal twenty-four-hour days about four thousand years before Christ, geologists now estimate the earth to be between five and six billion years old.

Fundamentalists had followed one of two ways to get the requisite amount of time into the Biblical record. The gap theory inserted the time between verses one and two of Genesis 1. God had made an original creation billions of years ago. Then a catastrophe befell it, and it became "formless and empty" (v. 2). Beginning in verse 3, we have a description of a re-creation which God performed in six twenty-four-hour days, about six thousand years ago.

Fundamentalism's other prime strategy was to account for the time by means of the flood, at which time conditions were set up which radically altered the earth. Under great pressure, layers of rock were laid down which would ordinarily take long periods of time to form. Thus, the earth *appears* to be much older than it actually is.

The new evangelicals have abandoned both the gap and the flood theories. The most popular alternative among them is the age-day theory, which maintains that the days in the record of creation in Genesis 1 are not twenty-four hours but long periods of indefinite length. Whereas fundamentalism had taken the word "day" (*yom* in the Hebrew) in its most literal meaning, the new evangelicals note that it also is used with other meanings, and they feel that the idea of an indefinite period of time is the most adequate for the explanation of the Genesis passage. There is a general correlation between the six creative days of Genesis and the geological periods.[20]

While Ramm indicates that this was the view which he held for a long time, and he still has great respect for it, by the writing of *The Christian View of Science and Scripture* he had moved to what he refers to as the "pictorial-day theory." He notes that there are some elements in the account which cannot be fitted into a purely chronological order—in particular, the sun and the stars are not created until after the appearance of light, the earth, and plant life. Ramm therefore suggests that the creation was not performed in six days, but was *revealed* in six days, or under the form of six days. In a series of pictures God made known to the writer of Genesis the general facts of creation. The grouping may be partly chronological and partly topical. It is not to be taken as a precise description of the order of events, or of the amount of time involved. Ramm recognizes that any effort to interpret the word translated "made" in Genesis 1 as meaning "showed" gives a rather artificial meaning to the text.[21]

Undoubtedly, the most troublesome problem in the relationship between science and the Bible has been biological evolution. Many fundamentalists assumed that the Hebrew word *min,* translated "kind" in most English versions, was to be equated with the biological concept of species. God had at the beginning created all the species which we now have, and these have remained fixed to the present time. Biology, however, claimed to have evidence that there had been a development of new forms from earlier forms. Fundamentalism's strategy therefore had been to combat evolution or development of any kind. Since the fundamentalist usually held that the flood in Genesis covered the entire earth, there were also some problems in getting at least two specimens of all of the present animal species (except fish and amphibians) into a ship with less than 35,000 square feet of floor space.

The new evangelicals hold to "progressive creationism" (Carnell terms it "threshold evolution").[22] This says that the word "kind" is not to be identified with "species." It is a general term meaning simply "subdivisions of." What God did was to create a broader grouping, perhaps on the level of the biological order. Over a long period, development took place through implanted laws or principles and new species arose. Then God initiated another kind, and more development occurred. There was evolution within each kind, but not from one kind to another.

The term "progressive creationism" is a good one. It is progressive in that it denies instantaneous creation and fixity of species, allowing for a moderate amount of development. It is creationism, however, because it denies that evolution has been total: God has created by a series of acts.

The new evangelical apologist believes that this view fits the scientific data quite well. The paleontological record reveals several gaps in which there are no transitional forms. These are generally at the level of the order. The evolutionist must either say that there have been transitional forms which have now been permanently lost, or that new forms arose spontaneously (by mutation) which were radically different from any prior forms. The progressive creationist feels that he more adequately accounts for these gaps by correlating with a series of acts of God, by which He made something quite new.

Ramm and Carnell have both indicated that theistic evolution is not totally contradictory to the Biblical account.[23] Theistic evolution teaches that God began the process by the first act of creation of matter and energy, and perhaps even life. He then worked creatively from within nature by immanent laws rather than by miraculous special creation. Man's physical makeup developed by a process of evolution. At some point, God took an existing animate form and by a direct creative act implanted in it a spiritual nature, referred to as a "soul," or the "image of God." Man therefore became qualitatively different from what he had been. While neither Ramm nor Carnell have in their writings indicated acceptance of this view, they indicate that a Bible-believing Christian could accept it if compelled by the evidence.

V

The Practical Application

PERSONAL ETHICS

For the average person, the really pressing questions in life are practical rather than theoretical. The problem to be faced is not, "What shall I believe?" as much as, "What shall I do?" The issues of ethics are inescapable.

Many different ethical systems have been produced in man's history. Some start from the idea that man is basically a part of the system of nature. Others emphasize man's reason and his uniqueness in relation to the natural world. Religions have generally also had something to say about right and wrong, good and bad. Christianity has especially addressed itself to questions of conduct.

In the ethical area, as in doctrine, new evangelicals consider the authority of the Bible a basic premise. God is believed to have spoken, and His Word is to be obeyed. Ethics is not a product of man's speculation. It is not constructed on the basis of man's best insight, observation and inference, but based upon truth communicated by God to man, truth which man could not arrive at by his own effort.[1] Natural man produces his ethical system not out of submission to God's will, but out of sinful rebellion.

The conflict between the Biblically revealed Christian ethic and the various systems of men's thought is not total. Natural man is not as wicked as he could possibly be, nor is his thinking about ethics completely incorrect. At various points secular ethics do agree with the ethics of the Bible.

As seen in the doctrinal section of this work, there is a general revelation as well as a special revelation. Available to all men is a partial knowledge of God's will; nature and history give indications of right and of good. Further, God has created all men in His own image.[2] There is, according to Romans 2:14, a certain law written on the hearts of men. This means that to some extent all men can, by looking within, know right from wrong.

The conception of an inward law is contested by many. Conscience, they say, is simply the result of conditioning, of parental inculcation. The diversity in content of the many moral codes in the world also challenges such an interpretation. Yet all men do seem to have a conviction that the distinction between right and wrong, good and bad, is genuine rather than merely personal prejudice. Despite all the variations among ethical systems, there is not total disagreement, and some points are held in common by all of them. No society in the world, for instance, holds that it is right to murder wantonly one's best friend. The moral image of God in man involved this thrust of distinction between right and wrong. It also apparently meant some specific content.

With the fall of man and the sin of individual men, the image of God became sullied, as Henry puts it. Man is now in opposition to, or rebellion against, God. His ability to recognize the moral truth is affected. When he reflects about right and good, his inward bias leads to distortion of the truth. Because the image of God has not been totally destroyed, there are glimmers here and there of the true ethic, but sin does mean that there are points of confusion and conflict.

Sin also means that man tends to reject revelation because it shows him his true condition before God. Just as some people avoid going to the doctor for fear that he will give them an unfavorable diagnosis, so man prefers to construct his own ethical philosophy, rather than adopt the Biblical teaching about his condition.

Biblical ethics is not opposed to philosophy. Indeed, it is revelation which alone supplies philosophy with a secure starting point.[3] Once these presuppositions are granted, the process of philosophizing can and should begin, and the superior consistency of the Christian view as contrasted with other options can be seen. Evangelicals are sceptical of a rational ethic being constructed by man's unaided effort, but optimistic about the possibilities when special revelation is brought in.

Not only does sin make it difficult for man to recognize the good, but it also interferes with his ability to do it. Much humanistic and idealistic ethics had assumed that man was basically good and could perfect himself by his own effort. Perhaps the ultimate of this was the little formula proposed by the Frenchman, Emile Coúe, "Every day in every way, I am growing better and better." The new evangelicals take issue strongly with all such views. The world is a fallen world. There are real forces of evil at work in it, and in particular there is a personal embodiment of evil called "the devil" or "Satan." There is a great moral drama going on in the world, a struggle between the forces of God and of the wicked one. Satan is engaged in tempting men, seeking to induce them to follow him in wicked thoughts and deeds. This means that man is simply not able either to know the good or to do it, apart from divine aid and energizing.

Ethics as traditionally conceived has usually said, "One ought to do thus and so," and, "One ought not to do such and such." What is the basis of this "ought"? Is it that man ought to do certain things and follow certain courses of action because they will bring happiness or pleasure to him, or to the maximum number of persons (and in the maximum amount)? That would be an anthropocentric ethic, based upon a study of man and his makeup, needs, and wants. It would also say that man is the highest value, that what promotes his welfare is good, and what detracts from it is bad. This makes the standard or criterion of ethics immanent within the world of nature and history, and within man's experience. Within this shifting world of flux, however, it is difficult to derive or establish any sort of objective basis for moral judgments. Everything is relative.

In a certain small town the telephone operator received a call each morning from someone asking her the correct time. She always cheerfully supplied the information. After several months, her curiosity became unbearable and she finally asked, "Do you mind if I ask who you are?"

"Oh," said the caller, "I'm the man who blows the whistle at noon and at six o'clock each day, and I always want to be sure that I have the correct time."

Chagrin was apparent in the operator's voice when she

said, "Why, I've been setting my clock by your whistle for
months!"

This is the problem of naturalistic ethics, as the new
evangelicals see it. There must be some objective basis of
right and wrong which goes beyond the varying opinions
and tastes of different men. They are not denying that there
are relative factors in ethics. The correct time is always the
correct time *somewhere;* there is no absolute time that is the
correct time at all points on the earth's surface. It is not
appropriate to ask, "What time is it on the sun?" Nonetheless, at a given spot on the earth's surface there is one time
which is correct for all people in that area, because there is
some objective factor, the position of the sun, which is relative to the situation. Similarly, the good is the good in a
particular situation, and might not be the good in a different situation. If this is to be the good for anyone in such a
situation (however finely defined), it must be based on something which goes beyond that specific set of circumstances.

The new evangelicals find an objective basis for ethics.
Right and wrong are not correlated primarily to man; they
are derived from the nature and will of an eternal, un-
changeable God, as He has revealed them to man.[4]

God's will is in itself the determiner of good. It is not
subject to any standard beyond itself. Some philosophies
and theologies have regarded "the good" as something external to God and given to God, something to which He
must conform. On the other hand, "voluntarists" such as
William of Occam maintained that God was utterly free
and arbitrary in what He willed. God could have willed
what we ordinarily now refer to as evil and it would have

been good simply because He willed it. God, if He chose, could have been what the Bible pictures the devil as being, and that would have been right.

According to the new evangelicals, God is in no sense subject to a standard of good outside of Himself and more ultimate than Himself. At the same time, this is not simply arbitrary. God wills and acts in conformity with His nature. There are some things that He is really not free to do, such as lying. This objective basis of good is not external to God, however; it is the very way He is. The moral activity of God is a revelation and closer definition of His nature. The will of God is therefore the basis of determination of the good.

The emphasis upon the primacy of duty, or doing what God wills and commands is, on the surface, in conflict with seeking one's pleasure or happiness. Yet, on closer examination, the antithesis is found to be artificial. Following God's will results in the maximum happiness and satisfaction for the doer, because what God wills is actually the greatest good for man, although it may not appear so in advance. Further, the person finds that as he does God's will, God gives him a satisfaction in the process of the doing. On the other hand, the person who gives himself to the pursuit of his own happiness finds frustration and boredom. Even as Jesus said, "Whosoever will save his life shall lose it; but whosoever shall lose his life for my sake and the gospel's, the same shall save it" (Mark 8:35, KJV).

We have seen that, for the new evangelical, ethics is serious business. It is not a matter of expediency or of self-fulfillment, primarily. It is rather a question of the will of the sovereign, holy God, which is not a trifling matter.

There is also a certainty and an authority about ethical standards, and they have not merely been derived from man's judgment. They have been revealed by God and are not subject to debate. They are to be accepted and obeyed. Such an ethical system is dependent upon special revelation.

While we will not attempt to discuss specific points of ethics, something of the content, or at least the framework, should be noted. The first principle is that love is the divine imperative in personal relations. The Christian has a responsibility to emulate God in his relationships with others. This means that he is to be characterized by love for both the non-Christian and the Christian.[5]

This love is *agape,* the kind of love which cannot be generated by man's will or effort, but is produced only by God. *Agape* does not seek the other for what it can get from him; it asks what it can do for him. It does not seek its own good at the other's expense; it seeks the other's good, even if at its own expense. It does not love because of the attractiveness of the other; it loves even despite the repulsiveness of the other.

An example from human experience might be a mother rushing into a burning home to rescue her child. The child may be ugly and unruly. By his disobedience, he may have proved to be a source of frustration to the mother, and may have driven her almost to desperation. Yet, without concern for her own welfare, the mother saves the child. That is a rough example of *agape* love, the kind of love God has shown. He did not love us because we were so attractive, or could do so much for Him, or because we first loved Him. The Bible teaches that God loved man while man was in rebellion and was spiritually weak and disabled.

Agape love is to be extended to all men, to those who hate as well as those who love us. It is easy to be nice to those who do good to us, but in Matthew 5:44 Jesus said that one was to love his enemies as well as his friends. He said in Luke 10:27 that the law could be summarized in two great points: to love the Lord your God with all your being; and to love your neighbor as yourself.

The illustration of this latter precept was the story of the Good Samaritan. The man the Samaritan helped was of the Jews, with whom his own race had bitter conflict. There was nothing appealing about the stricken man, and there was considerable danger, inconvenience, and cost involved in helping him.

But is love the only principle of human relations in the Christian ethic? Is it enough to say, "Practice love; there is no other norm"? The school of thought known as "situation ethics" says that this is indeed the case. There are no fixed norms other than *agape* love. There are no other moral absolutes. Potentially, anything is right if it is the most loving thing to do in that situation.

This principle has been applied in a number of theoretical situations. In its popular form, known as "the new morality," situation ethics has said that premarital sexual intercourse is justified by love, arguing that where there is genuine love, premarital sex is good and right. While the new evangelicals have not undertaken a comprehensive analysis and critique of situation ethics, they have elaborated this particular point.[6]

While love is the basic principle underlying the entire law, it is given its definition and content by the law. In the nature of God, love and righteousness are equally ultimate, and love is self-defining. In man, even redeemed man not yet fully sanctified, it is not self-defining, however. It is necessary for man to have some specific rules to give guidance to love. This has been done through God's moral revelation. God has definitely prohibited fornication and adultery. *Agape* love would not lead to premarital intercourse. It would prohibit it, since such sexual practice shatters the divine framework of sexual morality, leading to feelings of guilt and an actual estrangement from God. Love and law are not antithetical: love is the formal principle; law is the defining content.[7]

What is the place of the law in the Christian ethic, and what is its relationship to the gospel? It is extremely important to see that the law is not, and has never been, a means of salvation. It was not given in order that man, by perfectly fulfilling it, could satisfy God and thus deserve salvation. It was, rather, given to instruct man in righteousness, to make him aware of his sin, and to turn him to God for redemption. In Jesus Christ the requirements of the law have been fulfilled on behalf of the believer. The law, however, is the transcript of God's moral nature, and therefore is still the standard of conduct, both for the believer and the unbeliever.[8]

It is not the keeping of the precepts that the New Testament condemns, but the spirit of legalism that is repudiated. Legalism is keeping the law in all its minuteness and with the attitude that nothing more is required. It is an attitude of relationship to the law itself, rather than to the One who gave the law and stands behind it.

When this writer was a young boy, ice cream was a rare

luxury in the home. When a pint was brought home from the grocery store, it was divided into five equal portions. Frequently disputes arose among the three children who were home as to the exact equality of the portions, one maintaining that another had gotten more than he. On one occasion, this young man took a ruler, laid it alongside the brick of ice cream, and measured it into five exactly equal portions. That was legalism. Legalism in religion is not the keeping of precepts, but the exact adherence to the law, doing no more and no less than the law requires, and then regarding oneself as just. Giving a tenth of one's income to the Lord is not legalism. Giving $890.43 and not one cent more because one earned exactly $8,904.30 is legalism.

The New Testament lays down a number of rules, some positive in character and some negative, yet it does not attempt to give rules for all of life. There are several general principles, though, which are to be applied to the various situations of moral decision and action in which the Christian finds himself. Some of these may be enumerated.

The Christian's life is one of liberty in grace.[9] He is not bound by a legalistic conscience. Nothing that God has created is unclean by itself, nor when used in accordance with the Creator's intention. The problem with legalism is that the person who abstains may actually be every bit as worldly as the person who indulges. Inner attitudes as well as external actions are important, according to Jesus. It is the responsibility of the believer in his own relationship to God to determine what is appropriate, or right, and what is wrong.

Such liberty is to be guarded against the abuse which is

termed "license." [10] The purpose of the believer is to glorify God, and such practices as militate against that purpose are wrong, and ought to be avoided. Here is a proper limitation upon Christian liberty. The constitution of our nation and particularly the Bill of Rights guarantees each member of our society certain freedoms. Yet my freedom to swing my fist ends just short of my neighbor's nose, according to the law. Similarly, Christian liberty is bounded by the Christian's responsibility to glorify his God.

The Christian also has a responsibility to his fellow men, both the non-Christian and the weaker Christian.[11] Any action that would impede or hamper another's spiritual welfare and progress ought to be avoided. He does not live in a social and spiritual vacuum; he lives in a society, and consequently must gauge his conduct by the impact for good or for ill that it makes upon others.

Here the contrast with fundamentalism's separatistic ethic can be most clearly seen. Both Henry and Carnell have registered their protest against negativism, although Henry's renunciation was considerably less inflammatory in tone than Carnell's.[12] They are agreed in opposing fundamentalism's tendency to make certain practices wrong *per se*. Henry notes, for example, that in Biblical times dancing of a type was engaged in. Also, there seems to be no absolute condemnation of the use of wine, although drunkenness is certainly indicted. It is the circumstance and the degree of participation that makes these acts right or wrong.

Not that the new evangelicals advocate the practice of such activities, rather than avoidance of them. Quite the contrary is the case. What is objected to is the legalistic rejection of them as being inherently wrong. While some deeds (murder, adultery, and so forth) are clearly denounced in the Bible, others are not explicitly dealt with. Here it will not avail to substitute pulpit dogmatism for Biblical authority. Some actions are judged in the context of their contribution to the quality and effectiveness of the individual's Christian life.

The Christian is like an athelete in training. When he gives up certain practices, he does so not simply for the sake of giving them up, nor of restricting or truncating his life. He voluntarily surrenders certain areas of his life in order that he may develop to its fullest potential a particular area of his ability. The athlete abstains from eating some foods and engaging in late night life in order that he may most superbly do the one thing which is his purpose, *e.g.*, throwing a curve ball, kicking field goals, or running the hundred-yard dash. Similarly, the Christian may seem to be squelching his life. Jesus, however, said that He had come to give life, and to give it *abundantly* (John 10:10). Abstention from some activities enables the Christian to glorify God more fully, to imitate Christ, and to influence his fellow men.

To the outsider, the Christian life may seem to be like a circle, narrow and restrictive. The Christian is one who doesn't (or can't) do this and doesn't do that. To be sure, Christianity has often conveyed this image of itself. Rather, according to the new evangelicals, the Christian life is like a cylinder, the base of which is reduced as extraneous areas are eliminated. As this is done, however, the height increases as the believer grows in his one great primary pur-

pose: glorifying God. Development is in a dimension of life
of which the nonbeliever really knows nothing.

The fundamentalist is prone to regard avoidance of certain practices—drinking, smoking, movie attendance, card
playing—as tantamount to spirituality. Actually, the fundamentalist would probably deny this, but the tendency is
there. The danger lies in overlooking other greater sins,
such as anger, jealousy, hatred, gossip, and lust.

Separation should be not only a separation from sin and
the world, but primarily a separation unto God. The purpose of avoidance of evil is primarily in order to have an
intimate personal fellowship with the living God. The fundamentalist view of separation, if carried out consistently,
would mean cutting oneself off totally from culture. Radio,
television, the symphony, even baseball, would be illegitimate. The new evangelicals believe that the grace of God is
operative in cultural expression, that it restrains sin in its
worst manifestations and may even give expression to God's
truth. It is therefore at least potentially a legitimate field of
interest for the believer.

Positively, the Christian ethic, which is not based primarily upon a set of rules or laws, finds its standard in Jesus
Christ.[13] Even among non-Christians and those who would
not consider Him to be God in any unique sense, Jesus is
acknowledged as an outstanding person. His life seemingly
embodied moral perfection. There is, of course, the danger
that the imitation of Christ will become mere external copying. Rather, there is to be the inward molding of disposition
and thought into the likeness of Jesus. This becomes the
ideal of the Christian life.

But why does (and should) the Christian live the life of Christ? The primary motive is gratitude. Overwhelmed by a consciousness of what God has done in creating, saving, keeping, and providing for him, the believer responds by doing the Lord's commands and seeking to imitate Him.

The strength of the conservative's motivation for living is derived directly from his doctrine of salvation. The Christian does not live a good life in order to qualify for salvation, or even primarily out of a concern to extend the blessings of God to other men. He does so because of a profound sense that God has saved him, and that his salvation is something completely undeserved by him. Nor does he have the idea that by doing so he will be able to repay God fully and come to a point of merit rather than continuing to stand in grace. It is simply that gratitude is the natural response to grace, as revealed by the fact that both words come from a common root.

This is not only the basis for the specific deeds of personal righteousness of the individual, but also of his acts of loving concern manifested toward his fellow man. It would be wonderful if Christ still walked upon earth, and the Christian could bathe His feet, invite Him in to a meal, allow Him to sleep in his home, or give Him a cup of cool water, perhaps even at the cross. Then there would be adequate expression for the love and gratitude which he feels toward his Saviour and Lord. Such is not possible, for He is no longer here in physical presence. Jesus, however, indicated that doing such acts of kindness to another person was accounted the same as if it were done unto Him. He said, "Inasmuch as ye have done it unto one of the least of these my brethren, ye have done it unto me" (Matthew 25:40, KJV).

Robert C. Newell tells of a man traveling at night over an unfamiliar road when his car began to fail him. Finally it stopped. As he sat in his stranded automobile, wondering how he would proceed, another driver came along and offered help. The second driver had a tow rope in his trunk, and slowly and painfully he pulled the first vehicle thirty miles to a garage. Gratefully, the first man offered to pay his rescuer, but the latter steadfastly refused. Finally he said, "I'll tell you what you can do. If you really want to show your gratitude to me, you get a tow rope and keep it in your car all the time, and use it." This is the nature of a Christian's service to others. Jesus said, as He sent His disciples forth, ". . . freely ye have received, freely give" (Matthew 10:8, KJV).

Other motives are also mentioned in the Bible. In particular, the promise of rewards for obedience and the threat of punishment for disobedience. There appears to be something of a conflict between the reward motivation and the motive of gratitude. How are they reconciled? [14]

First, we should note that failure to consider the place of rewards would be to ignore, or perhaps even to doubt, one aspect of the Biblical teaching regarding the nature of God: His faithfulness in granting rewards.

Second, the reward motivation is never associated with the idea of inherent merit. Jesus did not teach that a faithful and obedient man can expect or even demand that God must do a certain thing for him. The reward is beyond what might be deserved. Furthermore, the reward is not always in accord with man's judgment of the comparative desert. This was particularly made clear by Jesus' teaching on the laborers in the vineyard, where those who began work at the eleventh hour received the same amount as those who came at the beginning of the day (Matthew 20:1-16).

Finally, it should be noted that self-oriented motives cannot be completely excluded, nor should they be. Even the person who is able to say that he lives as he does, not out of expectation of reward, but because of gratitude to God, is in danger of self-centeredness of even a stronger sort: he may pride himself on following virtue for its own sake rather than for rewards. Thus, whether the idea of recompense is introduced or excluded, the tendency to self-concern cannot be escaped.

The demands of the ethics of the new evangelicalism, like those of fundamentalism, are severe and stringent. Who can possibly fulfill them? To be holy as God is holy, to imitate the sinless, perfect Christ, to glorify God completely—these are beyond the imagination and certainly beyond the ability of man. It is precisely here, however, that the evangelical ethic makes its strongest thrust. The Christian life is not simply a matter of precepts; it is basically a life of power. The Holy Spirit is the dynamic of the Christian life.[15]

The Christian ethic is the ethic of the regenerate man. While the requirements of God are incumbent upon all men, God does not intend that man will be able to fulfill them simply by trying. Rather, when a person accepts Christ as Saviour, an amazing change called "regeneration" takes place. There is a new desire to live a godly life. Furthermore, at this new birth, the Holy Spirit comes to reside within the believer. Jesus told His disciples in Acts 1:8 that when the Holy Spirit came they would receive power—moral and spiritual power. The promise was fulfilled at Pentecost.

Somehow the Holy Spirit has a direct access to the mind and will of the believer. The very thoughts and life of Jesus are directed through the life of the person. Paul could say that it was no longer he who lived, but Christ who lived in him. This is the power that enables the Christian to live the Christian ethic. While recognizing that no one perfectly fulfills the standard within this life, there is the encouragement that it need not be dependent upon the resources of the person himself.

SOCIAL ETHICS

During its long history orthodox, or conservative, Christianity had stressed the application of its message to social ills. In the nineteenth century, for example, evangelicals in America were in the forefront of the forces contending for abolition of slavery.

As the twentieth century moved on, however, fundamentalism neglected this emphasis. To the non-evangelical observer it appeared that the fundamentalist simply had no social program. The fundamentalist seemed to be the modern equivalent of the priest and Levite, by passing suffering humanity.[16]

It is not difficult to see why the observer could gain this impression. Evils abounded in twentieth-century American Society. There was aggressive warfare, racial hatred and intolerance, liquor traffic, and friction, bitterness, and exploitation in relationships between labor and management. Numerous organizations were engaged in trying to combat these social ills. Some of them were religious groups, such as the World Council of Churches and the Federal Council of Churches of Christ. To the secular onlooker the fundamentalist might have been expected to lend his support to such worthy efforts. Instead, fundamentalists for the most part resisted, repudiated, and criticized the social efforts of both secular and liberal religious groups.

Fundamentalism opposed these group efforts because most of them were predicated upon the assumption of the essential goodness and moral capability of men. Problems of a social nature were the result of environmental factors or difficulties generated by society itself. If these factors could be eliminated, the problems would be solved. But fundamentalism believed that social evils derived from the sinfulness of individual persons. Society's difficulties could not be permanently solved unless there was a transformation of its members. The radical evil in man could only be overcome through individual appropriation of the redemption accomplished by Jesus Christ. It was not the end (the alleviating of injustice and suffering) against which the fundamentalist was protesting, but the means to that end. This would have made sense if the protest had been accompanied by an equally forceful assault upon social ills. If the removal of these social problems by relatively naturalistic means was not the solution, such a conviction could have been demonstrated by an aggressive program of social concern within a distinctly supernatural framework. Such did

not seem to be forthcoming, however. It was largely a negative protest of the wrong approach, without the proposal
of any real alternative.

The fundamentalist did not fail to take evil seriously—on
the contrary, it was he who saw man as completely corrupt,
and sin as a radical offense in the sight of God. But his
protest was very largely against sin in its individual
dimensions.

Fundamentalism was not absolutely silent on these social
matters. The liquor traffic, for example, came under attack,
and fundamentalists were strongly active in the prohibition
effort. Whether one feels that theirs was an effective approach to the solution of the problem, it was at least an
effort. Even here the phenomenon was treated more as an
individual than a societal ill, but the treatment of individual
sins involved at least an indirect coming to grips with the
broader issue. In most areas, however, little was heard from
fundamentalism on social ethics.

The first major thrust of the new evangelicals was a call
for a reversal of this trend in fundamentalism. If conservative Christianity were to become a really acceptable alternative for large groups of Americans, it must return to the
social dimension of its message which had been present
earlier. Otherwise it would become merely a tolerated
minority, or would assume cult status.

Carl Henry insisted that the evaporation of humanitari-
anism was in no sense implied by conservative theology.
Although there was belief in the total depravity of man, it
ought not to lead to pessimism. While sin is the "sickness
unto death," as Kierkegaard termed it, it is a curable dis-

ease. The gospel was regarded by the conservative as an infallible solution to the sin problem, if accepted by man.

Indeed, Henry would insist that only in the conservative view of man and sin could there really be optimism about world problems. Liberalism, with its idea of man's basic goodness, was not capable of really coming to grips with the problems. Neo-orthodoxy, by contrast, seemed almost to regard man as essentially sinful. Orthodoxy saw man's sinful condition and nature as the result of the fall and of man's voluntary choice, and thus as curable.

Not only the view of man, but the doctrine of last things sometimes was incorrectly interpreted, leading to conclusions which were anti-activistic in character. Both premillennialists and amillennialists believed that conditions would ultimately become worse prior to Christ's return. This was not based upon any doubt regarding the efficacy of the gospel, when it was accepted. Rather, it appeared to them that the Bible taught that there would be a certain lack of response. There would not be total conversion of the human race to faith in Jesus Christ. Yet, while this would mean that social evils could never be completely eradicated, it ought not to have precluded making a legitimate effort to eliminate society's corruption so far as possible.

The problem, as Henry, Ockenga, and others saw it, was that fundamentalism had overreacted against liberalism. Because liberalism had been preoccupied with the social gospel, fundamentalism had tended to neglect the social emphasis. Because liberals had used the wrong means in dealing with social ills, fundamentalists largely avoided any thrust against social evils.

The fundamentalist reaction stressed those aspects of Christianity which liberalism had neglected, which in turn produced an oversight of those very themes which the liberals were heralding. Thus, the spiritual dimension of man's life was undoubtedly the most crucial. To be well-fed and well-clothed in this life would be little comfort to a man whose soul would suffer endlessly in hell. While that was the most important aspect of life, it was not the only important factor. Jesus indeed said, "For what is a man profited, if he shall gain the whole world, and lose his own soul?" He also spoke of the value and importance of giving a cup of cold water in His name.

Thus fundamentalism more and more became an unbalanced theology and religion. The Bible seemed to speak of the Kingdom as having two dimensions, or aspects, one present and one future. Liberals stressed the "Kingdom now" character and talked about "bringing in the Kingdom." Fundamentalists majored increasingly on the "Kingdom then" or futuristic nature of the Kingdom. The Kingdom is both future and present, the new evangelicals insist, and it ought to be preached in both respects.

Evangelicalism must regain its social concern. Fundamentalism seemed to the new evangelicals to have divorced two aspects of religion which in the Bible and in the history of Christianity had generally been conjoined: doctrine and practice. In the New Testament Epistles of Paul, for example, doctrine is never taught abstractly, for merely intellectual consumption; doctrinal exposition is always followed by ethical application.

To understand the strength and the true motivation of

the new evangelical burden, one must remember that in common with other conservative theologies, it takes as its supreme and final authority in matters of belief and practice, the Holy Scripture. The primary thrust for an evangelical social ethic therefore does not come from an analysis of psychological and social factors, or from a conviction that it is necessary for the maintenance of evangelicalism's status. New evangelicals believe that the Bible teaches that there are social implications of the gospel, and social responsibilities of the Christian church.[17]

There is the example of Jesus Christ Himself. Much of His activity was the declaration of the gospel of salvation by faith in Him. The concern was for the specifically spiritual needs of men, yet a large portion of the accounts of His life describes His care for the physical needs of those who came to Him. In particular, He healed the sick and restored sight to the blind. On at least two occasions He miraculously fed great multitudes of people, and He even provided refreshments for a wedding feast. The two spheres of His ministry are especially linked together in Mark 2:9 (KJV), where He said to the lame man, "Thy sins be forgiven thee," and "Arise, . . . and walk."

It may be contended that Jesus' purpose in performing miracles of benevolence was to certify His divinity and thus bring about belief in Him. His ministry to the bodies of men was merely a means to attain the end of saving men's souls. This aim was certainly intended in many cases, yet it is doubtful whether it was the sole reason or even the major reason in every instance. Jesus is described as being moved with compassion as He saw the needs of persons. The Greek verb used here is a very vivid one in which emotion was felt not merely with the "heart," but with all of the visceral organs. Evidently at least some of His healings, or "benevolent miracles," were performed simply to relieve suffering and need.

The Christian is to follow the example of Jesus, to be like Him. I John 2:6 (KJV) says, "He that saith he abideth in him ought himself also so to walk, even as he walked." Therefore, Jesus' deeds of merciful kindness to those in need ought to be practiced by His disciples.

Another teaching suggested that the basis of discrimination of true believer from false at the final judgment will be practical deeds of service. As Jesus described the great judgment in Matthew 25:31-46, the Son of Man is pictured as sitting upon His throne. All peoples will be gathered before Him to be judged. Like a shepherd dividing sheep from goats, He will proceed to put some, the elect, at His right hand, and will send them into the eternal life prepared for them. Those on His left hand He will send into "everlasting fire," the punishment prepared for the disobedient.

Let us note the ground of this judgment. The elect inherit the Kingdom because they have fed Him when He was hungry, given Him drink when He was thirsty, clothed Him when He was naked, and visited Him when He was sick or in prison. When they ask when they have done all of these things, He says, "Inasmuch as ye have done it unto one of the least of these my brethren, ye have done it unto me" (Matthew 25:40, KJV). The unrighteous are judged on the basis of not having done these things.

Two observations emerge:

1. Deeds of compassion and mercy done to anyone are equivalent to ministering to Jesus Himself.

2. Such practical activity is regarded as the criterion of worthiness for the Kingdom.

Taken solely in abstraction from other Biblical teaching, the passage from Matthew 25 might be regarded as teaching that salvation is by works rather than by faith, which would seem to conflict with numerous other passages. A more adequate interpretation would be to say that salvation is only by faith, but that genuine faith will be evidenced by the presence of works, particularly works of mercy and kindness to those in need.

This also is the thrust of James' Epistle. His seeming tirade against faith is really a repudiation of the pseudo-faith which consists of intellectual assent without commitment of will and consequent action. Works identify the true faith as distinguished from the imitation.

James presents a hypothetical case. Suppose there is a brother or sister who is naked or destitute of food. If you wish him good luck in finding food and clothing, but don't do anything to help him, what good do you do? So, says James, faith without works is dead. The combined teaching of these passages is that if a person truly has saving faith, concrete deeds of kindness and mercy to others ought to be evidenced.

Still another passage (Matthew 22:37-39, KJV) is Jesus' reply to the question of what was the great commandment in the law. Jesus answered, "Thou shalt love the Lord thy God with all thy heart, and with all thy soul, and with all thy mind." The second commandment, He said, is like unto it: "Thou shalt love thy neighbour as thyself." The entire law and prophets could be said to hang, or depend, upon these two principles.

Just what was involved in this latter command to love one's neighbor as oneself? On another occasion a lawyer came to Jesus, asking what he must do to inherit eternal life (Luke 10:25-37). Jesus asked him what he read in the law, and he replied with the answer, based upon Deuteronomy 6:5 and Leviticus 19:18, "Thou shalt love the Lord thy God with all thy heart, and with all thy soul, and with all thy strength, and with all thy mind; and thy neighbour as thyself." Jesus commended him for his answer, instructing him, "This do, and thou shalt live." When the young man asked, "And who is my neighbour?" Jesus told the famous parable of the Good Samaritan, thereby not only answering the immediate question, but also defining what love really meant.

The Good Samaritan who loved his neighbor ministered to the needs of the wounded and robbed man. He treated the man's wounds, placed him on his own donkey while he himself walked, took him to the inn, and told the innkeeper to care for him, assuming all the expenses involved. Thus, the fulfillment of the command to love one's neighbor as oneself involved not merely sentimental feelings toward the other person—it meant actual acts of kindness and help.

John also deals with the matter of love (I John 3:14-18). Suppose, says John, that a person who has this world's goods sees his brother in need; yet, as John puts it, he "shutteth up his bowels of compassion from him." How can it be that the love of God dwells in him?

Helping others, removing suffering, evil, and injustice, are appropriate results of true faith in Jesus Christ and commitment to His purpose. The Bible does teach the necessity of Christian social responsibility.

There are two major areas of social concern: social welfare, aimed at alleviating the needs and problems of men; and social action, primarily concerned with reforming the basic conditions which are creating the problems. An instance of the former would be providing food and shelter to poor or deprived persons. The latter would be illustrated by effort, either legal or otherwise, to combat poverty or unemployment, or to prevent catastrophes. The new evangelicals agree that the Christian church has a stake in these matters. The means of implementing this concern is a further matter.

With respect to social welfare, there is much which can and should be done by the local church as well as by the denomination of which it is a part, and even by interdenominational fellowships—homes for the aged; children's homes; ministries to alcoholics, indigents, and others; adoption agencies; day-care nurseries; community centers; hospitals; chaplaincy programs. These might be termed church-sponsored welfare.

There are other agencies of social welfare which are not directly sponsored and controlled by church organizations as such. While the church is less directly involved, there nonetheless is opportunity for participation and referral.

Difference of opinion appears among evangelicals in the question of state welfare programs. Should the church regard the unemployment, retirement, and disability provisions made by the state and federal governments as fulfilling the function which the church once cared for? Should the church accept, welcome, or even encourage the increasing welfare function of the state, or should it resist, advocating other means for the provision of needs? Is the support of governmental welfare programs the fulfillment of the Christian's social responsibility?

Carl Henry represents the right wing of the movement on this matter. He strongly opposes the extension of the state's care for men's needs. The state's welfare programs cannot take the place of the church-sponsored program, for it fails to meet several of the criteria of Biblical social concern.[18]

Primarily, social welfare from the Christian standpoint must be regenerative: it must bear a testimony to Christ. This a state program cannot do. True, some denominations have distributed as part of their welfare program surplus goods received from the government. This is either an illegitimate use of public funds to forward religious testimony, and therefore a violation of separation of church and state, or it will lead eventually to the secularization of the church. Christian welfare work, Henry argues, seeks by its witness to restore men to relationship and fellowship with God. If it does not confront men with Christ, it may as readily desert them to Marx. Welfare which only alleviates man's material needs without caring for the spiritual is incomplete.

Furthermore, Christian social welfare must be personal. The direct contact between the donor and the recipient is largely lost in the impersonal relationship of a bureaucratic agency and the person who, rather than being an individual, is merely a number on a file folder or a set of holes punched in an IBM card. Withholding from a paycheck a certain amount of money which eventually goes to pay someone's unemployment dole is scarcely a fulfillment of the command to help one's brother, Henry feels.

There is a real danger in the Christian's feeling satisfied that through his effort or contribution to state welfare his responsibility has been satisfied. This approach can become a substitute for any real involvement with persons, just as Christians can in some cases give generously to support evangelistic missionary work on the other side of the world, while doing little or nothing to evangelize their next-door neighbor.

Finally, Christian social concern must be voluntary. There is little virtue in one's participation in a type of welfare in which taxes are by law assessed and withheld from his income. Whether he desires it or not, this is then used to provide social welfare. Although the Christian himself may favor this arrangement, and may have actually worked for the passage of the bill making it possible, he is advocating that another's money be involuntarily used for welfare purpose.

To Henry, an even greater danger is that the state, by coercing men to do their duty, can also force them to do what is not their duty at all. He thinks of the Amish, who declined to participate in Social Security because it had always been their practice to care for their aged themselves. The federal government, however, took their property and sold it at auction, using the proceeds to pay their Social Security taxes.

One of the points of Henry's objection to social welfare legislation is seen in his view of property rights. To him, social legislation attempts to level all men economically. It endeavors to eliminate poverty and to do it by virtually attempting to eliminate wealth: by taking from those who have more and distributing it to those who have less. Thus, it is violating the property rights of those from whom money is taken. The state is failing to fulfill its major role: the preserving of society and protecting of rights. It is not preserving the right of the one group and it is seeking to provide not only the needs or the due of the other, but their wants as well.

A different and more liberal view of the state's part in welfare is proposed by David Moberg in his book *Inasmuch*.[19] The church today cannot possibly take care of all the needs of society, he says. Society is too complex, people too mobile, and the church too small a minority. Nor have government welfare programs arisen because of the church's neglect or failure to meet its obligations. Moberg feels that a good case can be made for saying that these have grown out of the church's having done its work in welfare areas.[20] The diffusion of Christian values of mercy and love has made favorable attitudes toward social legislation.

Moberg goes further than that. He feels that social legislation is actually one of the ways in which Christians can fulfill responsibilities of love. He says that "Christian compassion is evident in cheerfully paying taxes to help meet welfare needs as well as in voluntary contributions to charities and gifts to specific persons in need." He feels that Christians ought in particular to work for the extension of social insurance programs. Until some better alternative is proposed, social insurance seems to him to be the practical program which is nearest to the "Christian ideal."

One can see the point of Henry's concern, lest the Christian seek to discharge his responsibility of compassion by some alternative means which does not really meet the standards of Biblical charity. Suppose that the need for works of Christian kindness were removed. Assume that, as a result of state welfare programs, there were no sick, hungry, and poor. Would that be an undesirable situation? To put it another way: Are the deeds of Christian love and mercy important in themselves, or only in view of the problems which do exist, and which did exist in Biblical times?

Henry's view of the function of the state seems to be that it exists to preserve social order rather than to transform it.[21] He cites what he calls four strategies of social transformation: revolution, reform, revaluation, and regeneration. He feels that regeneration is the only really acceptable and practical strategy. This requires the conversion and transformation of individual men, morally and spiritually, and a consequent transformation of society through the unleashing of a supernatural force. The strategy of reform seeks to change society by enforcing a different kind of behavior upon men. In the ultimate analysis, though, law cannot coerce love. Only from within can the kind of change be made in men about which he is concerned. The state's proper role is to preserve law and order and to administer justice.

This last thought leaves the door open for state effort in the area of social action. Here Henry's attitude toward the 1964 civil rights bill, while it was still under consideration in Congress, is instructive. It was evident that he favored the bill, because it was an attempt to preserve and guarantee rights and to administer justice. Yet, the law itself would not be sufficient to solve the problem. There must still be a change of attitudes, which law cannot effect. There must be the proclamation of the gospel as the means of changing men's hearts even on a matter such as civil rights.

But what is the role of the church in legislation? Both Henry and Moberg, representative of differing segments of contemporary evangelical thought, agree that the church ought not to be involved in the support of specific items of legislation.[22] Evidently the federal government feels this also, as witnessed by the Internal Revenue Department's challenging the tax-exempt status of *The Christian Century* even as this book was being written. The charge was that the periodical engaged in political activity in opposing vigorously the candidacy of Barry Goldwater in the 1964 presidential campaign, as well as in supporting concrete items of legislation.

Rather, the church has more indirect influence which should be exerted. It is the responsibility of the church to proclaim moral principles. The principles of social order enunciated in the Scriptures must be declared. Further, the church should encourage its members to become actively involved in the civic and political life of community and nation. It is through the activity of informed individual Christians that society will be influenced and laws enacted.

UNITY

One of the most conspicuous aspects of the Biblical teaching regarding Christian believers is that all who are in Christ are somehow one. Jesus prayed for those who believed in Him and were to believe in Him, that ". . . they may be one, even as we are one" (John 17:11, RSV). Paul's reference to the church as the body of Christ stresses that, despite the diversity of gifts and roles, the church is one.

Yet when one looks at the religious scene he sees the church existing not as one but as many. Christianity is divided into Protestant, Eastern Orthodox, and Roman Catholic. Even within Protestantism in America there are nearly 300 separate churches, denominations and sects, and the number is increasing.

The problem becomes even more evident when examined on the local level. In the small midwestern town of Centreville, four churches stand at the intersection of Main and Church streets. On Sunday morning, four congregations partially fill the four old buildings. Members of the different churches compete for the few parking spaces on the street. Four poorly-paid ministers carry on their work, preaching basically the same message, believing primarily the same doctrines, and administering struggling programs which are repetitive and competitive. At the denominational headquarters of the groups to which these local churches belong, the same story of duplicated effort is found. How does one reconcile the Biblical teaching regarding the unity of the church with such apparent diversity?

The usual way of handling the issue is through the distinction between the visible and invisible church, which has already been expounded in the chapter on doctrine. Unity is on the level of the invisible church, and is therefore spiritual unity. All who believe in the same Lord and Saviour are one, which is not inconsistent with the many churches.[23]

Nonetheless, there may well be disunity on the level of the local churches. The new evangelicals are disturbed by certain tendencies in what they call "independency." Independency is simply the movement to have status as churches apart from connection with other individual churches or ecclesiastical groups. Usually, independency is accompanied by creedalism, or the requirement of belief in doctrinal statements. The danger lies in stressing this more and more strongly, elaborating the points more finely. In the ultimate form, one can only have fellowship with or work together with those who agree on even the minor points of doctrine.[24]

Sometimes independency leads to withdrawal from those with whom there is no real doctrinal difference, but rather a dispute on the basis of personality or minor creedal items. The later history of fundamentalism was characterized by this tendency; the Presbyterian Church is a good example. When Machen and others found themselves out of harmony with the foreign missions program of the Presbyterian Church, U.S.A., and with Princeton Seminary, they organized their own mission board and their own seminary and eventually were expelled from the denomination. They founded what they believed to be a "true" Presbyterian Church, the Orthodox Presbyterian Church. Soon other divisions followed. A group led by Carl McIntyre withdrew and founded the Faith Seminary and the Bible Presbyterian Church. Soon Faith Seminary was also rent asunder and Covenant College and Seminary was founded in St. Louis. The continued splintering of conservative Christianity has brought disrepute upon the church.

Should a Christian never separate from the church? The new evangelicals feel that where there is definite apostasy, the Christian must withdraw. Carnell says a Christian should remain in the fellowship unless he has compelling reason to withdraw, which was particularly the case with the group which gave him spiritual birth, just as Paul ministered to the Gentiles only after he had first preached the gospel to his fellow Jews. Division in the church should not be multiplied needlessly.

What are the criteria as to whether the church is still a church or has become apostate? Carnell states three. First, is the gospel taught in the official creed or confession of the group? The official stand, rather than the views and lives of individual members, ought to be the determining factor. Second, is the gospel free? Is an individual preacher permitted to declare the gospel? Finally, is there opportunity to protest abuses, and to dissociate oneself from denominational declarations? [25]

There are only two justifiable grounds for separation from an existing denomination: eviction or apostasy. The new evangelicals are not separatists in the sense of seeking to withdraw from any slight taint of heterodoxy or worldliness.

What is being done in a positive way to promote unity? There are several efforts to bring at least cooperative action among evangelicals, both those who are within denominations involved in the conciliar movement (National Council of Churches and World Council of Churches) and those outside. There is the National Association of Evangelicals, together with its commissions and subsidiary agencies; membership in it is not precluded by affiliation with a conciliar group. There is the World Congress on Evangelism, held in Berlin in October and November, 1966, and, with a somewhat narrower spectrum of involvement, the Congress on the Church's Worldwide Mission, at Wheaton College in April, 1966. Periodicals like *Christianity Today* help to establish liasion among evangelicals, as does Intervarsity Christian Fellowship on the collegiate level in both Britain and America.

What of the evengelicals' relationship to the conciliar movement, the National and World Councils? [26] Carl Henry estimates that between one-fourth and one-third of the membership of these groups is made up of evangelicals. He feels that the ecumenical leaders, if they really desire to see evangelicals participate enthusiastically in ecumenical discussions, could take certain steps. These would include giving evangelicals within the movement a proportionate voice and representation in the leadership. There should be a stress on Biblical evangelism, the central authority of the Bible, and Biblical or divinely given principles of conduct. What he is seeking is not a complete conciliation to evangelical principles. He is asking that consideration be given to evangelicalism, so that its voice would be adequately heard.

The new evangelicals desire to engage in conversation with non-evangelicals. They see the complete withdrawal of some conservatives from contact with non-conservatives as unwise and unbiblical. There may well be sincere and earnest seekers after truth in various groups. If conservatives have the truth, then there is value in discussion with others; there is a confidence that the truth will ultimately prevail. The willingness to write for *Christian Century* is an example. Some feel that there is value in being in the ecumenical movement for the sake of dialogue. This would be particularly desirable under conditions such as those mentioned above.

But what of church union, the joining of presently existing denominations in organic merger? There are churches whose separate existence derives not from doctrinal differences, but from sociological, racial, or cultural differences, and these ought not to remain separate and divided. They should seek, wherever possible, to unite with other churches of like convictions.[27]

Organic union must be based upon a common doctrinal conviction, however. Doctrine does divide, and it always will. An attempt to obtain visible union where there are differences on major theological points will lead only to confusion and greater disunity. Henry thinks it strange that some who urge organic union on the basis that the Bible teaches the doctrine of the unity of the church overlook the fact that the Bible teaches with equal vigor several other doctrines as well. The churches whose separate existence is based on differences of theology ought to seek to resolve them by discussion, and most of all by submitting to the authority of the Bible as being God's revealed Word and will. The tendency to minimize doctrine is one major weakness of the ecumenical movement. The new evangelicals favor efforts toward reunion of separate denominations, although this is not absolutely essential for spiritual oneness of the body of Christ, the church. This unity must be on the Biblical basis of doctrine. Further, there should be a realistic awareness that complete organic union is not likely to be realized in history.[28]

The willingness to remain in contact and cooperative
activity with those of somewhat different theology is seen
most dramatically in the evangelistic campaigns of Billy
Graham. For some time Graham has accepted invitations to
hold crusades from committees made up of more liberal
clergymen as well as conservatives. Liberals have held positions of leadership in the local planning, and have participated in the program. For this, Graham has been severely
criticized by some extreme fundamentalists. He is not accused of perverting the gospel, but he is criticized for associating with non-evangelicals. The fundamentalists believe in what they call "secondary separation," meaning that
it is not sufficient to be separated from the world and that
one must also be separated from those who are not themselves separated. Graham is believed to be placing his approval upon liberalism by being associated with liberal
men. He is sending converts back into liberal churches.

While Graham himself has been careful to avoid replying
to these criticisms, a number of his associates and sympa-
thizers have. One of the most extensive answers is *Cooperative Evangelism,* by Robert Ferm,[29] in which the author
points out that, corrupt and incorrect as were the temple
and synagogue of Jesus' day, He did not withdraw from
them. He was not afraid to be seen associating with publi-
cans and sinners if that would help Him to win someone.
Ferm notes also that other great evangelists, such as
Wesley, Whitefield, Finney, Edwards, Moody, and Sunday
were not separatists in the strict sense.

The new evangelical sees a strange inconsistency in the
strict fundamentalist's reasoning. If, as the latter claims, the

liberal is not a regenerated Christian, is he not as much in need of salvation as any other sinner? If involving the leadership of liberal churches in a crusade will bring members of these churches to hear the gospel, is this not a very desirable thing? To be sure, converts do return to liberal churches, in many cases. They are followed up, however, through an intensive campaign. Rather than fearing that their spiritual fervor will falter when they are in contact with theological liberalism, the new evangelical is hopeful that the converts will become leavening influences in their churches.

There is one further dimension to the ecumenical movement. With the beginning of the Second Vatican Council in October, 1962, there has been an increasing interest in discussion between Roman Catholicism and Protestantism. The new evangelicals have watched the developments with great interest. Henry is hopeful that there may possibly be another reformation stirring within the Roman church, and feels that the increased interest in the Bible is particularly encouraging. There ought to be inter-faith conversation, yet this must sooner or later deal with the major issues of doctrine, and preferably sooner. In particular, the matter of the status of the Pope would have to be examined. Reunion could take place only if there were satisfactory treatment of those issues which occasioned the original Reformation, and there is little evidence thus far of any real change of Rome's mind on this. Particularly disappointing is the indication that only by return of the "separated brethren" could there be a satisfactory ecumenical development.[30]

VI

Conclusion

GENERAL CHARACTERISTICS

Having surveyed the new evangelicalism in its several areas
of expression, we may now make some observations about
the movement.

Basic to the entire structure is the view of two cognitive
revelations of God which are harmonious with one another.
Consequently, there can never be any conflict between the
Bible, properly interpreted, and natural knowledge, correctly construed. If all the data were available, a perfect
harmony would emerge. This means also that it is possible
to exhibit the truthfulness of the Biblical view by appealing
to evidence drawn from the created space-time universe.

This conception of the general revelation also produces a
positive attitude toward culture. The new evangelicalism
believes that even the unbeliever is exposed to God's truth
and thus may unknowingly give expression to it. Whereas
fundamentalism had been rather culture-rejecting, the new
evangelicalism is culture-affirming. Although the truth and
its expression may be distorted as a result of sin, it is nonetheless to be found in various places.

There is a reaffirmation of the authoritative status of the Bible as a special revelation from God. It is a genuine, rational, cognitive, and informational revelation. Having been given completely from God, it is fully truthful in its assertions and can be depended upon. It is trustworthy.

Yet the true purpose and function of the Bible must be seen. It is neither a textbook on science nor a guidebook of history. Its basic message is religious, or theological. Its role is to bring man into fellowship with God. References to science are merely incidental to the primary purpose, yet, where they do occur, scientific assertions are true.

The Bible bears the impress of its culture upon it. Revealed truth came through the culture of its day and must be interpreted within that context. Biblical meaning and truth must be evaluated in terms of the usages appropriate to the time of the writing, not those of the twentieth century.

The status of the Bible as an authority is also clear. Its teachings give the basis for belief and for conduct. While it may not be completely explicit, or detailed, in every case, inferences can be drawn from principles laid down in the Bible.

What of reason? Since reason is utilized to evaluate and interpret the Bible, and to determine whether it is really true, is not reason, rather than the Bible, actually the ultimate authority? Some critics have maintained that here is an inconsistency.

There are, indeed, two authorities—reason and the Bible —but they are different types of authorities. While the new evangelicals do not use the terms, it might be appropriate to refer to the Bible as *the legislative authority,* and to reason as *the judicial authority*. Man is not capable of producing or arriving at the content of belief or ethics by his unaided ratiocination. He needs the revealed truth supplied by the Bible. God has made known what is true and what is right or good.

While the Bible not only states what is true, but also that its content is true, one cannot utilize it as his authority in this latter sense. He must decide on the basis of the evidence whether the claimed revelation is genuine. He is forced to do so on the basis of reason, whether he wishes to or not. In actual practice, all men do this, regardless of how naïvely or simply it may be done. This is not in conflict with the Bible's authoritative function. It is not giving the content of one's faith; it is simply determining whether the Bible is what it claims to be. If one does not make his decision on this basis, he runs the risk of following whatever impulse may happen to occur at a given moment.

This also sheds light on the question of faith and reason. Faith must precede, in the sense that one cannot antecedently produce the content of faith, nor establish it by something more ultimate. When a man is willing to accept the revelation provisionally, however, and trace out its implications, its reasonability can be seen. One begins with faith, but moves on to understanding.

The new evangelicalism has also insisted upon the social emphasis of its gospel. Here again we may note that this theology is not as exclusively other-worldly as was fundamentalism. While the most important concern must be for evangelism—that is, the eternal spiritual destiny of man—it must not be to the neglect of man's more temporal needs. Man's suffering must be alleviated, his needs cared for.

Here, also, a broadened conception of common grace reveals itself. God is able to work through organizations and institutions which are not expressly Christian. The Christian may and should cooperate with them, if they are the most efficient and appropriate means of carrying out the social responsibilities of his faith.

The new evangelicalism is less sharply separatistic than its forerunner, fundamentalism. Whereas fundamentalists in the nineteen twenties and thirties were separating from denominations which had become liberal, and were organizing separate denominations, the new evangelicals advocate remaining within the parent denomination unless it has become completely apostate. Here the conservative may exert a leavening influence, may engage in theological dialogue with his more liberal counterpart.

The broader view of separation also means that the new evangelical believes in utilizing whatever means of evangelism become available to him, again as long as no essential compromise of doctrine is involved. If he can minister to a larger group of unsaved persons by cooperating with ministers of more liberal persuasion, he will do so. In this, he sees himself as following in the pattern of Jesus. The new evangelical does not believe that the Biblical teaching on separation requires him to cut himself off from contact with those whose theology may not be completely orthodox.

One of the claims made by the new evangelicals is that they are continuing the earlier tradition of fundamentalism as represented in *The Fundamentals,* and that later fundamentalism was actually a narrowing and a distortion of that tradition. From their published writings it appears that the new evangelicals hold to all of the fundamentals: the inerrancy of the Bible, the virgin birth of Jesus, the substitutionary atonement, the deity of Christ, the bodily resurrection, and the bodily future second coming of Jesus. At the same time there is a reluctance to demand consensus on relatively secondary issues of theology, as later fundamentalists did. There is no uniform position required on the millennial or tribulational issues in eschatology. There are some divergences on the exact nature of inspiration and inerrancy of the Bible. There is an openness to theistic evolution as a real and valid option for the conservative Christian.

In this the new evangelicals appear to be closer to the fundamentalism of 1910 than were the later fundamentalists. The articles in *The Fundamentals* were written by men with a breadth of theological positions. Both pre- and postmillennialists contributed to them. James Orr, a theistic evolutionist, was one of the writers. Not only did later fundamentalists reject Orr's views on revelation and evolution, but such views would not have been regarded as possibilities for one who would be orthodox. The breadth of viewpoint within the new evangelicalism is not a departure from the initial character of the fundamentalist movement, but a return to it.

The new evangelical theology has not committed itself too definitely on the issue of Calvinism versus Arminianism. In this it is much like fundamentalism, which embraced both streams of orthodox theology. The new evangelicalism appears to be, as Bernard Ramm has put it in classroom lectures, "a Calvinism of mood, rather than a Calvinism of system." Systematic Calvinism, the theology of the *Insti-*

tutes of the Christian Religion and of the Synod of Dort, had definite and powerful tenets. These are best summarized in the famous TULIP acrostic: Total depravity, Unconditional predestination, Limited atonement, Irresistible grace, and Perseverance of the saints. One does not find this systematic structure in the new evangelical theology, partly because these men have not really applied themselves to these issues.

The Calvinistic mood may be observed in the view of sin. Sin is regarded as radical, and the debilitating effect of sin upon the natural powers of man's reason is marked. This is seen clearly in Carnell's *Apologetics,* for instance. Still this consequence of natural depravity is mild when compared with a really strong Calvinism. Compare, for instance, Carnell's *Apologetics* with Cornelius Van Til's *The Defense of the Faith*. In this latter work, a thorough-going Calvinism virtually eliminates common ground in the sense in which Carnell speaks of it.

Trends Within the Movement

As any movement grows and develops, it begins to show certain trends, some of which may even be reversals of earlier positions.

One noticeable development is a growth away from the initial somewhat exclusively apologetic orientation and toward greater doctrinal formulation. In an editorial in 1962, Carl Henry expressed himself on this subject. While it is necessary and important to argue for the truth of the Biblical revelation, he said, a theology which is always concerned with this will never really reach its goal of developing the message. Instead of always giving account to other disciplines, theology ought to call them to account. He felt that the current failure to produce strong dogmatics was largely a result of such excessive preoccupation. This also gives the impression that God's truth must be defended or made respectable, as if it did not have its own intellectual compulsion.[1]

The shift in emphasis can also be seen by examining the literature. Particularly is this true of the writings of Bernard Ramm. His first several books were all apologetic in character: *Problems of Christian Apologetics, Types of Apologetic Systems, Protestant Christian Evidences,* and *The Christian View of Science and Scripture.* The only real exception was *Protestant Biblical Interpretation,* his second book, but even that had an indirect apologetic thrust. *The Pattern of Authority* is a transitional writing. Three later works are more definitely doctrinal-didactic in character: *The Witness of the Spirit, Special Revelation and the Word of God,* and *Them He Glorified.*

The strong apologetic emphasis in the early days of the movement may well have been needed by a new school of thought seeking to establish itself in the theological world and the intellectual universe in general. Now that the new evangelicalism has apparently attained considerable recognition, it is reasonable to assume that we will see a greater amount of doctrinal activity.

Another interesting development is the apparent delineation of the movement into subdivisions. As might be expected in a movement of this type after twenty years, positions of more conservative and more liberal standpoint have begun to appear. These are not to be regarded as schisms, but simply as differing convictions on some matters. Having a profound distaste for the fragmentation which has so often characterized fundamentalism, the new evangelicals are not likely to part company over their differences.

One of the most easily recognized of these differences is that of Henry from Carnell and Ramm on biological evolution. Henry feels that the other men go too far in their attempt to reconcile Biblical statements with the findings of empirical science. He does not believe that science's conclusions are so firmly established that theology ought to conform to its present pronouncements.[2]

Henry is also critical of the terminology employed by Ramm and Carnell. The use of terms like "progressive creationism" and "threshhold evolution" involves certain dangers. Either needless concessions are being made to evolution, or there is an element of deception in the terminology. The contemporary evolutionist is led to believe that there are broader areas of agreement between himself and the Christian than actually exist. Because there are certain irreconcilable differences between Biblical theism and evolution, the apologist must clarify them or run the risk of either compromising Christian theology or gaining a merely verbal truce.[3]

It is in his *Case* book that Carnell appears farthest to the left of any of the new evangelicals. It is likely that he was overstating himself to those of a more liberal persuasion, and it is difficult to determine how much of his statement is to be interpreted hyperbolically. In the book he is so strongly critical of fundamentalism and so open on the matters of biological evolution, the antiquity of the human race, and historical errors in the Bible, that his position appears to have shifted considerably from the *Apologetics.* In that earliest work, Carnell even referred to himself as a fundamentalist.

The harsh tones of Carnell's book even prompted a negative reaction from Ramm as he reviewed the work.

> His treatment of the fundamentalists will call forth a very strong reaction from them, and I would remind the good author that the fundamentalists, for all the shortcomings they might have, are still members of the Church.[4]

If we were to classify the men upon whom we have primarily concentrated in this work, we would find Henry the most conservative, Carnell the most liberal, with Ramm somewhere in between (probably closer to Carnell than to Henry). This may be the result of Carnell and Ramm moving farther to the left, and Henry less so. For example, in 1947, following the publication of Henry's book *The Uneasy Conscience of Modern Fundamentalism,* the periodical *United Evangelical Action* printed the best letter supporting the book and the best letter opposing it. The latter was written by Bernard Ramm, who maintained that the ethic which Henry proposed could not and should not be extended to the unregenerate world; it was for the church only. Some see Henry as having become more conservative with passing years, finding evidence of this in the editorials in *Christianity Today,* particularly those dealing with matters of social ethics. To some extent this may be true, since even in his first book Carnell used the expression "threshold evolution," but without complaint from Henry at the time.

Other developments are rumored, but cannot be substantiated from published material. As a result of reactions to his *Case* book, Carnell seems to have moved back toward a more conservative position, particularly on Biblical inspiration and inerrancy. Some of the early members of the Fuller Seminary faculty have departed, with some protestation of theological trends within the school. A reference in an article in *Evolution and Christian Faith Today* speaks of some "new evangelicals" in the American Scientific Affiliation who hold to theistic evolution, but this is not documented.[5] There seems to be a greater doctrinal diversity within the new evangelicalism now than at its inception.

REACTION FROM THE RIGHT

As might be expected, the reaction of fundamentalism (or of conservative theology to the right of the new evangelicalism) has been mixed, but largely negative. Some criticisms have been *ad hominem* in character. One critic said of the new evangelicalism that it is a movement born of compromise, nurtured on pride of intellect, growing on appeasement of evil, and doomed by the judgment of God's Holy Word. Other criticism has been more directly concerned with the issues themselves.

One area of criticism is theology. Some see the move-

ment as failing to emphasize all of the areas of theology. To
some extent this may be correct, but may grow out of the
reasons suggested at the beginning of the chapter on doctrine. The new evangelicals' willingness to settle for broad
consensus rather than detailed agreement in some areas
such as eschatology has come in for criticism. In the Colorado Conservative Baptist Association, the Denver Conservative Baptist Seminary is criticized by some because of
tolerance on the millennial issue, and an unwillingness to
require a pretribulational or even premillennial commitment. According to these critics, the post-tribulationist is
denying the plain teaching of Scripture. To tolerate post-
tribulationism is therefore to deny, in effect, the inspiration
of the Bible, and will undoubtedly lead later to other departures from the orthodox faith. The critics evidently feel
that some positions, such as premillennialism, and even
pretribulationism, are clearly and explicitly taught, whereas
the new evangelicals regard them as less definite.[6]

Cornelius Van Til of Westminster Seminary has also criticized the latitude of the new evangelical theology. In particular, he feels that Arminianism is tolerated, rather than a
clear Reformed, or Calvinist, position being enunciated.
Here, again, while most new evangelicals are of a Calvinistic persuasion, they are not as convinced as Van Til that
the Reformed theology is unequivocally the Biblical view.[7]

The same objection carries over into Van Til's appraisal
of the new evangelical apologetics. Van Til believes that the
very essence of man's sin rests in his autonomy. Man believes he is sufficient both morally and intellectually. He can
recognize truth by his reason, so he need not submit to

God. Yet sin has obscured man's understanding and belief in God's truth. He must admit his own error and accept what God has said about his status. He must submit himself to the authority of the Bible, because God has said it.[8]

To Van Til, the apologetic method of his former student, Carnell, appeals too much to the unregenerate consciousness of the autonomous man. The effort to demonstrate the superior rationality of the Christian world-view is an appeal to the autonomous reason of sinful man. Man does not have to surrender his own judgment; he can see that the system is true. Yet this is an incipient denial of the very gospel which Carnell is preaching. If man is able to judge of the truth of the message, his reason evidently has not been very seriously damaged; he is not really totally depraved. Perhaps he is not really in need of salvation by grace, either. Van Til feels that Carnell's system is better than his method, but only because of inconsistency.

Apart from the question of whether Reformed theology is so definitely established as the Biblical view that one can criticize on the basis of whether another view agrees with it is another underlying issue. Van Til seems to hold that total depravity means being as sinful as one can possibly be, that the unsaved man is totally unable to recognize spiritual truth. On this basis, there is some question as to whether one should attempt to communicate with the non-Christian at all. Not all Reformed theologians would take this approach of Van Til's, however.

Some Conservative Baptists have criticized the philosophy of education of the Denver Seminary. At Denver, the evangelical convictions are submitted to a critical compari-

son with alternative views, both religious and secular. This
the critics equate with the Harvard philosophy that "reasoned heresy is better than unreasoned orthodoxy." The
trusting minds of students are submitted to a mixture of
Biblical truth and the "doubts and questions of the sin-
warped minds of the world's heathen philosophers." The
assumption seems to be that the various views are presented
on an equal footing, with the student left to choose, without
any guidance or critique by the instructor.[9]

The area at which the sharpest criticism is aimed is Billy
Graham's cooperative evangelism. The complaints have
dealt with a variety of points, the most common being that
Graham, by cooperating with liberal churches and ministers, and having even such men as Norman Vincent Peale
sit on the platform with him, is tacitly approving of the
liberalism which they represent. He is failing to distinguish,
for the public, the spiritual value of nurture in a conservative church from that of a liberal church. He is sending
converts back into liberal churches, where their spiritual
zeal will be confused and they will be given stones instead
of bread.

Van Til and those associated with him have also objected
to Graham's preaching as being too Arminian. It assumes
too much ability by man to accept salvation, to take the
initiative. Again, the issue is one of an extreme Reformed
position versus a less Calvinistic view.[10]

The attacks upon Graham have varied in intensity. Some
critics have been content simply to abstain from cooperation with his crusades; others have definitely opposed him.
An outstanding instance of the latter is Bob Jones Univer-

sity, where students are forbidden to pray for Billy Graham and his crusades, and where Bob Jones said that Graham had done more harm to the cause of Jesus Christ than any man alive.[11]

Not all fundamentalists are opposed to Billy Graham. Many who would not be classified as new evangelicals on the other points enumerated, nonetheless see Graham's work as blessed of God, and cooperate with and support it.

Fundamentalists have also criticized the new evangelicals' view of Scripture. Robert Lightner's charges include a willingness to interpret the Bible in the light of science, a hesitancy to use the term "verbal" with respect to inspiration, and an according of differing degrees of authority to various parts of the Bible.[12]

The estimation of the new evangelicalism, even among right-wing fundamentalism, ranges over several shades. The group associated with the Central Conservative Baptist Theological Seminary in Minneapolis seem to regard the new evangelicals as "half-hearted" heretics who really have more in common with neo-orthodoxy and neo-liberalism than with true fundamentalism.[13] Others, such as Lightner, consider them to be misguided brethren who should be prayed for and reasoned back into the truth.[14]

REACTION FROM THE LEFT

The reaction of more liberal thinkers has been more favorable. In part, this is probably due to the fact that the new evangelicals, while criticizing those to the left of them, and pointing out the distinctions between them and themselves, have done it in a more cordial and amiable spirit than did the fundamentalists. For the liberals, this has proved to be a welcome change, and has helped to foster dialogue.

One of the evidences of a more positive reaction by liberals is the recognition of the new evangelicalism as a valid theological option. After the time of J. Gresham Machen's writings, fundamentalism produced little that was sufficiently scholarly even to be considered in theological debate. Once again, however, the respect and hearing which Machen's thought formerly achieved is being accorded to the new evangelical theology.

William Hordern was one of the first to recognize the calibre of this rising theology. As early as 1955 he wrote sympathetically and appreciatively of the contributions made by Carnell and others. In his later works he acknowledged even further that these men were laboring to be scholarly, open-minded, and modern.[15] A generation earlier, conservative Protestantism would have been regarded only as a religious oddity rather than a scholarly theological movement. It is significant also that when Westminster Press wanted to publish a trilogy in which the dominant theological positions of the day would be allowed to speak for and defend themselves, Edward Carnell was selected to write one of the books.

Even periodicals of a more liberal character are welcoming interaction involving the new evangelicals. An instance of this was Carnell's article on "Post-Fundamentalist Faith" in *Christian Century*.[16]

When Karl Barth, in his tour of the United States, lectured at the University of Chicago, the panel which discussed his lectures included Carnell. Although Barth himself has referred to *Christianity Today* as "Christianity yesterday," it was felt that a new evangelical ought to be among those evaluating his thought.[17]

These various indications seem to justify the belief that the more liberal segments of Christianity are indeed regarding the new evangelicalism with a rather open attitude. It seems likely that there will be genuine theological interaction between these groups in the future.

But not all liberal reactions have been favorable. In particular, *Christian Century* has spoken out critically on several occasions. One was the Billy Graham New York City Crusade in 1957. An editorial entitled "Fundamentalist Revival" expressed real concern over the attempt of fundamentalism to become again a major force in American Protestant life. Fear was shown that if the effort were successful, it would "make mincemeat of the ecumenical movement, . . . divide congregations and denominations, . . . set back Protestant Christianity a half-century." [18]

While perhaps more fervent in tone than other criticisms of the Graham crusades, the editorial was representative in content of the negative reaction that has come to Billy Graham from some liberal spokesmen. The fundamentalism underlying the message is based upon a naïvely literal view of the Bible. To these liberals, the view of sin and the possibility of human transformation seems too shallow and Pollyanna-like—just believe, and your sins are forgiven, and you become a new creature. Further, acceptance of the five fundamentals is required for church membership, ministerial qualification, or cooperation with other churches or

denominations. While Graham himself does not insist upon
these distinctives, he holds them and becomes a powerful
force for the promotion of fundamentalism.

The *Century* was therefore critical of liberal ministers
who cooperated with the crusade. Desiring to see their
churches built up by using the dubious means employed by
mass evangelism, they fail to see the real dangers. The growth
of strength in fundamentalism threatens to be divisive and to
harm any real long-term ecumenics.

Another sharp criticism of the new evangelicalism was
an editorial in *Christian Century* entitled "Demythologizing
Neoevangelicalism." The public, says the article, sees neo-
evangelicalism primarily as a negative movement against the
ecumenical movement and against the social involvement of
mainline churches. The article seems to be a counterattack
against these criticisms, in which the neo-evangelicals are
accused of the same charges.[19]

The charge of the neo-evangelicals against ecumenism is
that unity is pursued at the expense of truth. There is an
attempt to coordinate the witness without having reached
complete agreement in all matters of faith. Yet, the *Century*
editor charges, the neo-evangelicals are "paraecumenical,"
striving for a type of ecumenical movement through the
National Association of Evangelicals. But if one were to
examine the doctrinal beliefs of any two evangelicals from
two denominations, he would find as great a diversity in
their views as among various members of the World Council of Churches.

The new evangelicals also complain that "non-evangelical
Christians" express themselves and take action as Chris-

tians on social, economic, and political problems. Yet, the neo-evangelicals are doing the same thing: they are speaking on socio-political issues. Even Billy Graham's sermons deal with these topics. Indeed, according to the *Christian Century,* the neo-evangelicals can be depended upon consistently to support any "nationalist-militarist" program of the federal government.

At least, says the editorial, it is now apparent that both movements are involved in ecumenism and in programs of social concern. It is now possible to ask openly which program is preferable and more productive. The editors of the *Christian Century* have, however, looked with favor upon developments in the new evangelical camp stressing the humanity of Jesus and the social application of the gospel.[20]

A CRITIQUE OF THE MOVEMENT

It is appropriate to attempt a critique, both positive and negative, of the new evangelicalism. This will be done largely from the perspective of its own presuppositions and the declared objectives which the movement has set for itself. It is scarcely fair to criticize a given theology because it has not fulfilled certain values espoused by another theology, unless one can establish that this is a value which all theologies should pursue. It is no mean task.

How well, then, have the new evangelicals accomplished their self-appointed task? It will be recalled that the movement arose out of a desire to avoid making the intellectual mistakes of fundamentalism, in which many of the results of modern scholarship were rejected and fundamentalism cut itself off from both the general culture and other streams of theology. The new evangelicals have striven to maintain that God's revelations of Himself in nature and in the Bible are fundamentally in harmony with one another. It has sought to state the Christian faith in an intellectually respectable fashion. It has endeavored to heal the schism between the theological right and left, at least to the point where meaningful theological dialogue could be pursued. It has striven to apply the gospel to the needs and problems of society.

Note that the new evangelicals' treatment of the intellectual problems has been a competent one. These men have prepared themselves through a thorough academic training to deal with the issues. Where they are not personally prepared to deal with a specific area of discourse, they have drawn upon the thought of scholars in that field. Thus, for instance, Ramm acknowledges that he is not a scientist, and that he is dependent upon those who are. When questions of Biblical criticism and allied issues are discussed, the original Biblical languages are used. It is when discussing philosophy that these men are actually most at home, since they have thorough academic training in that field.

They have isolated and treated the true problems. Whereas fundamentalism had often fallen back upon condemning secular knowledge as simply the evil workings of evil men, the new evangelicals have sought to deal with the actual issues.

The new evangelicals have taken an approach to science and the Scriptures which is intended to create harmony between science and theology. This has helped to remove some of the prejudice which scientists have at times held toward conservative Christianity.

They have also helped to relieve some of the unnecessary tensions between conservative theology and modern culture. Part has been achieved through an amplification of the distinction between inspiration and interpretation. For example, conflict between paleontological data and the interpretation of Genesis 1 has been alleviated by showing that identification of the Biblical "kind" with the scientific "species" is a matter of interpretation rather than inspiration. These insights have been gained both by exegesis of the Biblical original languages and by the application of proper hermeneutical maxims. At the same time, however, these men do not simply accept uncritically the pronouncements of science. Part of the removal of unnecessary conflict has resulted from a critique of the extension of science into areas where its application is illegitimate.

Another commendable aspect of the work of the new men has been their willingness to acknowledge frankly the presence of real difficulties. The chapter on "difficulties" in Carnell's *Case* book, for instance, is one of the most candid pieces of self-criticism in all of theology.

The new evangelicals have also inveighed against the indifference to social problems sometimes found in fundamentalism. They have noted the areas where work must be done and have suggested some of the Biblical teaching on the issues.

Further, they have helped to reestablish a sufficiently amiable relationship between themselves and the neo-orthodox and neo-liberals, so that there can now be discussion of theological differences. Their doctrine has become sufficiently respectable intellectually to cause those to the left to regard it as warranting examination and evaluation.

This has not been the only contributing factor, however. The willingness of the new evangelicals to discuss doctrinal differences with neo-orthodox and neo-liberal theologians represents a break with the past. The fundamentalists, with their strong conception of separation, probably would not write an article for *Christian Century* even if invited to do so. That would be a stigmatizing association with liberalism. Consequently, most of the theological output of fundamentalism relative to liberalism has been polemic in character rather than irenic. If there is to be some sort of reconciliation between divergent theologies in Christianity, there must be a mutual respect among the men who hold them. This the new evangelicals have helped to create.

Finally, these men have in certain areas of doctrine made good their claim to be a continuation, or resumption, of orthodoxy. They have claimed that fundamentalism is a departure from orthodoxy and that they, the new evangelicals, are merely returning to the true orthodox view. This appears to be true of Ramm's statement of the witness of the Spirit, which had come to be neglected by Protestant scholasticism and especially by fundamentalism. Ramm's view goes back to Calvin's formulation.

Another area where these men are closer to classical orthodoxy is eschatology. This is true not because of the presence of any precise millennial view, but because of the absence thereof. Orthodoxy had never stated any one millennial view to be a requisite of theological rectitude and spiritual fellowship. Fundamentalism has more and more demanded conformity to dispensational premillennialism. By their open approach to the issue, the new evangelicals have placed themselves in the older orthodox position.

Much in the new evangelicalism, from the standpoint of this writer, is commendable. Yet there are also several areas of apparent weakness in its theology, areas which will require more attention and better answers. Perhaps the most disturbing of these unsolved difficulties relate to the unity and antiquity of the human race. Here there is a considerable discrepancy between the pronouncements of anthropology and the amount of time which neo-evangelicalism is able to fit into the Biblical record. The approach seems to be that we cannot know for certain what the solution is, and that we ought not to attempt too close a concord at this point. This is undoubtedly a wise attitude to take, in view of the uncertainty of the data. Note, however, that on the new evangelicals' assumptions, this conflict ought not to be *permanently* insoluble. It seems that there should at least be some indication of the direction from which it is believed the solution will come. Will further study in anthropology reduce the estimated age of man? Will the requirements of the Biblical record be sufficiently expanded to allow for a greater antiquity? At present it does not appear likely that either of these alternatives will come to fruition, at least without the alteration of some of the principles of the new evangelicalism.

There is a need for continuing interaction with Biblical criticism, particularly New Testament-form criticism. George Ladd has published a volume on criticism which deals competently with a wide range of issues.[21] Everett Harrison's New Testament introduction volume concerns itself with critical problems, and Bernard Ramm has a short section on form criticism in his evidences text. Yet there will have to be continued wrestling with specific problems, and especially with the new quest for the historical Jesus.

In some other areas the new evangelicals do not seem to have kept abreast of developments. Noticeably, virtually nothing has been said on the problems raised by analytical philosophy. While these apologists have treated logical positivism and existentialism with considerable competence, the later forms of analytical philosophy, often referred to as "ordinary language philosophy," have moved beyond the position of logical positivism. The questions of meaning and verification raised by this philosophy do not seem to have really been adequately answered by the new evangelicals. Ramm has in three places indicated an awareness of the movement and the problems it has raised. In the preface to his work on special revelation, he indicates his debt to the professional linguists for showing him the inadequacy of some of his assumptions regarding language.[22]

In 1962, *Christianity Today* polled several scholars on the question, "What is the most critical issue that modern science poses to the Christian church today?" Ramm's answer was, "If science shows us how sentences assert and how they are verified or falsified, how is it that theological sentences assert and how are they verified?" [23] He also has drawn a parallel between Karl Barth's theology and analytic philosophy.[24] This would indicate an awareness by Ramm of the problem. In today's philosophical environment, however, an apologetic which attempts to establish a theology of transcendent truths must respond to the challenges regarding just how theological language asserts and in what way it is meaningful.

Nor has the new evangelicalism completely solved the issue of inerrancy of the Bible, either. To assert that the Bible is free from errors is meaningful only if there is a definite explanation of what is meant by an error. What would have to be present in the Bible in order for the new evangelical theologian to admit that there is an error? Until this is clearly delineated, all talk about inerrancy seems rather empty. That which cannot be disproved really cannot be proved, either.

There is a tendency toward elasticity of the word "inerrancy." One sometimes gets the impression, in reading Carnell's *Case* book, for instance, that he has sought at all lengths to preserve the word "inerrancy," but has so redefined it as almost to have lost the original meaning. The possible usage which he suggests seems particularly weak and subject to criticism. If inspiration simply guarantees an inerrant copying of what may be an erroneous source, inerrancy would be refuted only if the original source were available and discrepancy of the Biblical record from it could be established. The practical significance of the doctrine seems to have been lost.

There appears to be weakness in social ethics, also. Although the movement began on a clarion call for social application of the gospel, there seems to be more decrying of the fundamentalist neglect and more calling for a social ethic than its actual production. Principles have been laid down, but not a great deal has been done with the concrete problems of social evil. The editorials in *Christianity Today*, for example, tend to concentrate on problems such as race relations, the liquor traffic, or speeding drivers. On issues such as labor-management disputes there is some reluctance to commit. No great thrust in the matter of social welfare seems to have been forthcoming from evangelicalism, either. The effort needs to be increased if it is to be more than verbal.

There is also validity in the charge that the new evangelicalism has not developed a fully rounded theology. There is a real need for an up-to-date conservative work in systematic theology. Some of the major problems need to be dealt with in the light of recent research. For example, the sovereignty of God and the freedom of man ought to be related to recent research in the behavorial sciences. This is also true of the doctrine of original sin. The knowledge of God ought to be expounded for students who are exposed to existentialism. The work will be hard, and will require versatile theologians, but it is necessary. While the doctrines of the new evangelicals are not basically different from those held by the early fundamentalists, the intellectual milieu is quite different. Relating the timeless truths to yesterday's problems will not be adequate.

One of the prime objectives of the new evangelicals was to bridge the gap between fundamentalists and liberals, to re-establish communication between these two wings of the church. In this they have been only moderately successful to date. In their effort to open the channels of communication with those to the left of them, these men have in many cases lost their rapport with the fundamentalists. Carnell's *Case* book particularly incurred their wrath. This is the accurate insight of Clearwaters' article, "The Double Divisiveness of the New Evangelicalism." Many of the fundamentalists are now turning upon the new evangelicals the same type of criticism that they used on the liberals in the twenties. This is not true of all fundamentalists, however. While disagreeing with the new evangelicals, Lightner's book does so in a spirit of love and with a desire to bring reconciliation between them and the fundamentalists. The new evangelicals, he feels, are still brethren, and ought to be treated as such.

One cannot blame the fundamentalists completely for their lack of cordiality. The tone of Carnell's book was severe, and was scarcely calculated to stir good feelings among the fundamentalists.

The new evangelicals have greatly improved the climate of discussion with the neo-liberals and neo-orthodox. They have won the respect of these men, who regard their work as genuinely scholarly. It is difficult to determine how much the new evangelicals have succeeded in effecting any appreciable shift of liberal doctrine toward their own position.

THE FUTURE

What of the future of the movement? Is it possible to predict what developments will occur, on the basis of any discernible trends? While it may be difficult to make concrete predictions at this time, there are one or two areas on which attention ought to be focused for possible developments.

One will be whether the right and left edges of the movement will continue to move farther apart. As indicated, there are some noticeable differences in the matters of science, of social ethics, and of inspiration of the Scriptures which may actually develop into ruptures.

The new evangelicalism regards itself as a reaction from fundamentalism toward a more traditionally orthodox theology. This it seems definitely to be. At the same time, however, it has been moving in the general direction of neo-orthodoxy. Some fundamentalist critics maintain that it already has moved to an essentially neo-orthodox position. While to this author such does not seem to be the case, it will be a question whether, in introducing more subjective factors into its doctrine of revelation than had fundamentalism, it will move beyond orthodoxy to neo-orthodoxy. While there is a definite distinction between the two views at present, the gap could become smaller.

Furthermore, the methodology of the new evangelicals will bear closer examination. Carnell particularly has stressed the rational demonstration of the truth of the Christian world-view. He has appealed to a method which verified the Christian system like a broad hypothesis, much as does the scientific method. Van Til has suggested that this method is basically the same as liberalism, and Hordern has expressed the same estimate. It may be that, in the effort to bridge the gap between liberal and conservative, these men are endeavoring to combine two fundamentally opposed methodologies.

Still another difficulty in Carnell is the relationship of the internal, or innate, knowledge of God to the postulate of revelation. Which really is prior? Is there some kind of *a priori* knowledge of God, without special revelation? Some have found here an internal contradiction in Carnell's system. This innate knowledge of God has not really been developed since the *Apologetics,* however.

The movement is one with continuing vitality. The men who comprise it are still relatively young, and are well trained. Other bright scholars are appearing, and with specialties not present in the original group. There is an organization, the National Association of Evangelicals, which, though including other conservatives, represents quite well the general approach of the new evangelical movement. There is an articulate organ, *Christianity Today.* There is awareness of the movement by more liberal thinkers and even by the secular world. The future should be one of continuing strength and growth for the new evangelicalism, particularly if it gives its attention to some of the persisting problems which cling to it.

Notes

CHAPTER I

1. The intellectual problems facing orthodoxy in the twentieth century are discussed in William Hordern, *A Layman's Guide to Protestant Theology* (New York: The Macmillan Company, 1955); William Hordern, *The Case for a New Reformation Theology* (Philadelphia: The Westminster Press, 1959); Carl Henry, *Evangelical Responsibility in Contemporary Theology* (Grand Rapids: Wm. B. Eerdmans Publishing Co., 1957).

2. For the history of fundamentalism, see: Steward Cole, *The History of Fundamentalism* (New York: The Richard R. Smith, Co. Inc., 1931); Norman Furniss, *The Fundamentalist Controversy, 1918-1931* (New Haven: Yale University Press, 1954); Edward Rian, *The Presbyterian Conflict* (Grand Rapids: Wm. B. Eerdmans Publishing Co., 1940); Genevieve Forbes Herrick and John Origen Herrick, *The Life of William Jennings Bryan* (Chicago: Buxton Publishing House, 1925); Ned Stonehouse, *J. Gresham Machen* (Grand Rapids: Wm. B. Eerdmans Publishing Co., 1954).

3. *Bible Champion,* No. 32 (1926), pp. 503-4.

4. Furniss, *op. cit.,* p. 21.

5. William Hordern, *New Directions in Theology Today: Volume I, Introduction* (Philadelphia: The Westminster Press,

1966), pp. 75-76. For specific documentation, cf. *Yearbook of American Churches,* Herman C. Weber, ed. (New York: Round Table Press, Inc.), 1933 ed., pp. 300-05; 1939 ed., pp. 6-17; 1941 ed., pp. 129-38.

6. Harold Ockenga, "Can Fundamentalism Win America?" *Christian Life and Times,* Vol. II, No. 6 (June, 1947), pp. 13-15. Carl Henry, *The Uneasy Conscience of Modern Fundamentalism* (Grand Rapids: Wm. B. Eerdmans Publishing Co., 1947).

7. Edward Carnell, *An Introduction to Christian Apologetics* (Grand Rapids: Wm. B. Eerdmans Publishing Co., 1948). Carl Henry, *Remaking the Modern Mind* (Grand Rapids: Wm. B. Eerdmans Publishing Co., 1948). Bernard Ramm, *Protestant Christian Evidences* (Chicago: Moody Press, 1953).

8. Stanley High, *Billy Graham* (New York: McGraw-Hill Book Company, 1956).

9. Carl Henry, " 'Why Christianity Today?' " *Christianity Today,* Vol. I. No. 1 (October 15, 1956), pp. 20-21.

10. James DeForest Murch, *Co-operation Without Compromise,* (Grand Rapids: Wm. B. Eerdmans Publishing Co., 1956).

CHAPTER II

1. Bernard Ramm, *The Pattern of Religious Authority* (Grand Rapids: Wm. B. Eerdmans Publishing Co., 1957), p. 16.

2. Edward Carnell, *The Case for Orthodox Theology* (Philadelphia: The Westminster Press, 1959), p. 119.

3. Edward Carnell, *An Introduction to Christian Apologetics* (Grand Rapids: Wm. B. Eerdmans Publishing Co., 1948), pp. 156-157.

4. Bernard Ramm, *Special Revelation and the Word of God* (Grand Rapids: Wm. B. Eerdmans Publishing Co., 1961), chapter 2.

5. *Ibid.,* chapters 3-5.

6. Carnell, *The Case for Orthodox Theology,* pp. 35-39.

7. *Ibid.,* pp. 33, 41-43.

8. Carl Henry, *The Protestant Dilemma* (Grand Rapids: Wm. B. Eerdmans Publishing Co., 1949), p. 58.

9. *Ibid.*, pp. 58, 74, 103.

10. *Ibid.*, p. 120.

11. Carnell, *The Case for Orthodox Theology*, p. 108.

12. Bernard Ramm, *Special Revelation and the Word of God* (Grand Rapids: Wm. B. Eerdmans Publishing Co., 1961), p. 180.

13. Bernard Ramm, *Protestant Christian Evidences* (Chicago: Moody Press, 1953), Ch. III.

14. *Ibid.*, Ch. IX.

15. Bernard Ramm, *The Pattern of Religious Authority,* and *the Witness of the Spirit* (Grand Rapids: Wm. B. Eerdmans Publishing Co., 1957, 1959).

16. Everett F. Harrison, "Criteria of Biblical Inerrancy," *Christianity Today,* Vol. II, No. 8 (January 20, 1958), pp. 16-18. "The Phenomena of Scripture," *Revelation and the Bible,* Carl Henry, ed. (Grand Rapids: Baker Book House, 1958), pp. 235-50.

17. Carnell, *The Case for Orthodox Theology,* pp. 109-11.

18. Ibid., pp. 48-49.

19. Ramm, *Special Revelation and the Word of God,* chapter 8. Henry, *The Protestant Dilemma,* pp. 95-107.

CHAPTER III

1. The treatment of the knowledge of God and the entire doctrine of God is, unless otherwise indicated, drawn from Carl Henry, *Notes on the Doctrine of God* (Boston: W. A. Wilde Co., 1948).

2. Carl Henry, *Remaking the Modern Mind* (Grand Rapids: Wm. B. Eerdmans Publishing Co., 1948), p. 237; Edward Carnell, *An Introduction to Christian Apologetics* (Grand Rapids: Wm. B. Eerdmans Publishing Co., 1948), chapters 7 and 8.

3. Bernard Ramm, *The Christian View of Science and Scripture* (Grand Rapids: Wm. B. Eerdmans Publishing Co., 1955), pp. 322-25; Edward Carnell, *The Case for Orthodox Theology* (Philadelphia: The Westminster Press, 1959), p. 95.

4. Carnell, *The Case for Orthodox Theology,* pp. 96-97; Ramm, *op. cit.,* pp. 308-15.

5. Carnell, *The Case for Orthodox Theology,* pp. 95-96; Ramm, *op. cit.,* pp. 306-08.

6. The topic of the constituent nature of man is discussed in Carl Henry, *Giving a Reason for Our Hope* (Boston: W. A. Wilde Co., 1949), pp. 69-71; Carl Henry, *Christian Personal Ethics* (Grand Rapids: Wm. B. Eerdmans Publishing Co., 1957), chapter 4; Edward Carnell, *The Case for Orthodox Theology,* pp. 23, 129.

7. Carnell, *The Case for Orthodox Theology,* pp. 67, 72.

8. *Ibid.,* p. 72.

9. Henry, *Giving a Reason for Our Hope.*

10. Carnell, *The Case for Orthodox Theology,* pp. 66-68. Billy Graham, *Peace With God* (New York: Pocket Books, Inc., 1955), chapter 4.

11. Bernard Ramm, "Jesus Christ, Hallmark of Orthodoxy," *Christianity Today,* Vol. III, No. 22 (August 3, 1959), pp. 9-11.

12. Carl Henry, "Our Lord's Virgin Birth," *Christianity Today,* Vol. IV, No. 5 (December 7, 1959), pp. 9-10.

13. Edward Carnell, "The Virgin Birth of Christ," *Christianity Today,* Vol. IV, No. 5 (December 7, 1959), pp. 9-10.

14. Carnell, *The Case for Orthodox Theology,* p. 69.

15. *Ibid.,* p. 68.

16. *Ibid.,* pp. 69-71.

17. *Ibid.,* pp. 69, 73; Billy Graham, *op. cit.,* chapter 9.

18. *Ibid.,* pp. 23-32; Graham, *op. cit.* chapter 10.

19. *Ibid.,* p. 73; Graham, *op. cit.,* chapter 11.

20. *Ibid.,* p. 73.

21. *Ibid.,* p. 74.

22. *Ibid.*

23. Edward Carnell, "The Government of the Church," *Basic Christian Doctrines,* Carl Henry, ed. (New York: Holt, Rinehart and Winston, Inc., 1962), pp. 248-54.

24. G. S. S. Thomson, "Death and the State of the Soul After Death," *Basic Christian Doctrines,* Carl Henry, ed. (New York: Holt, Rinehart, and Winston, Inc., 1962), pp. 269-275.

25. Stanley High, *Billy Graham* (New York: McGraw-Hill Book Company, 1956), pp. 63-64.

26. George Ladd, *Crucial Questions About the Kingdom of God* (Grand Rapids: Wm. B. Eerdmans Publishing Co., 1952), pp. 65 ff.

27. *Ibid.,* pp. 77-81.

28. *Ibid.,* pp. 107-108.

29. *Ibid.,* pp. 122-23.

30. *Ibid.,* pp. 141-50.

31. George Ladd, *The Blessed Hope* (Grand Rapids: Wm. B. Eerdmans Publishing Co., 1956), chapter 3.

32. *Ibid.,* p. 91.

CHAPTER IV

1. Edward Carnell, *An Introduction to Christian Apologetics* (Grand Rapids: Wm. B. Eerdmans Publishing Co., 1948), chapter 4; *The Case for Orthodox Theology* (Philadelphia: The Westminster Press, 1959), chapter 2; Bernard Ramm, *Protestant Christian Evidences* (Chicago: Moody Press, 1953), chapter 1; Carl Henry, *Remaking the Modern Mind* (Grand Rapids: Wm. B. Eerdmans Publishing Co., 1948), chapter 8.

2. Ramm, *op. cit.,* p. 33; Henry, *op. cit.,* p. 232-33; Carnell, *Apologetics,* p. 89.

3. Carnell, *Apologetics,* pp. 91-101.

4. Ramm, *op. cit.,* pp. 33-34.

5. Edward Carnell, *A Philosophy of the Christian Religion* (Grand Rapids: Wm. B. Eerdmans Publishing Co., 1952).

6. *Ibid.,* chapter 3.

7. Ramm, *op. cit.,* p. 34; Carnell, *Apologetics,* pp. 56-58, 108-109.

8. Ramm, *op. cit.,* pp. 22-25, 34.

9. Ramm, *op. cit.,* Chs. 4 and 5.

10. Carnell, *Apologetics,* p. 252; cf., all of chapters 14 and 15.

11. Ramm, *op. cit.,* pp. 127-28; cf. Henry, *op. cit.,* chapters 4 and 5.

12. Ramm, *op. cit.,* pp. 34-35.

13. Carnell, *Apologetics,* pp. 161-64.

14. Ramm, *op. cit.,* p. 41.

15. Carnell, *Apologetics,* pp. 164-66.

16. Bernard Mayo, *Ethics and the Moral Life* (London: Macmillan and Co. Ltd., 1958), p. 39.

17. Edward Carnell, *Christian Commitment* (New York: The Macmillan Company, 1957).

18. Carnell, *Apologetics,* pp. 52-55.

19. Bernard Ramm, *The Christian View of Science and Scripture* (Grand Rapids: Wm. B. Eerdmans Publishing Co., 1954), chapter 2.

20. *Ibid.,* pp. 211-18.

21. *Ibid.,* pp. 218-29.

22. *Ibid.,* pp. 271-72; Carnell, *Apologetics,* pp. 236-42.

23. Ramm, *Science and Scripture,* pp. 280-93; Carnell, *The Case for Orthodox Theology,* pp. 94-95.

CHAPTER V

1. Carl Henry, *Christian Personal Ethics* (Grand Rapids: Wm. B. Eerdmans Publishing Co., 1957), p. 145.

2. *Ibid.,* pp. 148 ff.

3. *Ibid.,* p. 149.

4. *Ibid.,* chapter 8.

5. *Ibid.,* pp. 219 ff.

6. Carl Henry, "The 'New Morality' and Premarital Sex," *Christianity Today,* Vol. IX, No. 20 (July 2, 1965), pp. 21-23.

7. Henry, *Christian Personal Ethics,* p. 261.

8. *Ibid.,* chapter 14.

9. *Ibid.,* p. 420.

10. *Ibid.,* p. 423.

11. *Ibid.,* pp. 428 ff.

12. *Ibid.,* pp. 422-23, 434-36; Edward Carnell, *The Case for Orthodox Theology* (Philadelphia: The Westminster Press, 1959), pp. 120-21.

13. Henry, *Christian Personal Ethics,* pp. 529-30.

14. *Ibid.,* pp. 536 ff.

15. *Ibid.,* Ch. 19.

16. The discussion of this neglect by fundamentalism is detailed in Carl Henry, *The Uneasy Conscience of Modern Fundamentalism* (Grand Rapids: Wm. B. Eerdmans Publishing Co., 1947), and Harold Ockenga, "Can Fundamentalism Win America?" *Christian Life and Times,* Vol. II, No. 6 (June, 1947), pp. 13-15.

17. David Moberg, *Inasmuch* (Grand Rapids: Wm. B. Eerdmans Publishing Co., 1965), pp. 38-41.

18. Carl Henry, "The State in Welfare Work," *Christianity Today,* Vol. IV, No. 8 (January 18, 1960), pp. 21-23, and "Has Anybody Seen 'Erape'?", *Christianity Today,* Vol. 4, No. 8 (January 18, 1960), pp. 12-14.

19. Moberg, *op. cit.,* pp. 128-34.

20. *Ibid.,* pp. 106-07.

21. Carl Henry, *Aspects of Christian Social Ethics* (Grand Rapids: Wm. B. Eerdmans Publishing Co., 1964), pp. 110-11.

22. *Ibid.,* pp. 125-26, 130-33; Moberg, *op. cit.,* p. 127.

23. Editorial "Principles of Christian Unity," *Christianity Today,* Vol. IX, No. 9 (January 29, 1965), p. 29.

24. Carl Henry, "The Perils of Independency," *Christianity Today,* Vol. I, No. 3 (November 12, 1956), pp. 20-23.; Carnell, *The Case for Orthodox Theology,* pp. 114-17.

25. Carnell, *The Case for Orthodox Theology,* pp. 132-37.

26. Carl Henry, "Evangelicals and Ecumenism," *Christianity Today,* Vol. X, No. 17 (May 27, 1966), pp. 10-13.

27. Editorial, "Principles of Christian Unity."

28. Carl Henry, "The Perils of Ecumenicity," *Christianity Today,* Vol. I, No. 4 (November 26, 1956), pp. 20-22.

29. Robert Ferm, *Cooperative Evangelism* (Grand Rapids: Zondervan Publishing House, 1958).

30. Henry, "Evangelicals and Ecumenism," p. 13.

CHAPTER VI

1. Carl Henry, "The Evangelical Thrust," *Christianity Today,* Vol. VI, No. 9 (February 2, 1962), pp. 28-29.

2. Carl Henry, "Science and Religion," *Contemporary Evangelical Thought,* Carl Henry, ed. (Great Neck, N.Y.: Channel Press, 1957), p. 256.

3. *Ibid.,* pp. 250-51.

4. Bernard Ramm, "Sideswipes and Sidesteps," *Eternity,* Vol. X, No. 9 (September, 1959), p. 40.

5. Thomas D. S. Key, "The Influence of Darwin on Biology," *Evolution and Christian Thought Today,* Russell Mixter, ed. (Grand Rapids: Wm. B. Eerdmans Publishing Co., 1960), p. 29.

6. "Conservative Baptist Cross-Currents in Colorado," *Baptist Missionary-Evangelist,* Vol. XVII, No. 5 (May, 1962), p. 9.

7. Cornelius Van Til, "The New Evangelicalism," unpublished paper, pp. 35-39.

8. Cornelius Van Til, *The Case for Calvinism* (Philadelphia: Presbyterian and Reformed Publishing Co., 1964), chapter 3.

9. "Conservative Baptist Cross-Currents in Colorado," p. 10.

10. Van Til, "The New Evangelicalism," pp. 9-10.

11. "Graham in Greenville," *Christianity Today,* Vol. X, No. 13 (April 1, 1966), p. 44.

12. Robert P. Lightner, *The Saviour and the Scriptures* (Philadelphia: Presbyterian and Reformed Publishing Co., 1966), chapter 7.

13. William A. Ashbrook, "The New Evangelicalism—The New Neutralism," *Central Conservative Baptist Quarterly* (Summer, 1959); Richard V. Clearwaters, "The Double Divisiveness

of the New Evangelicalism," *Central Conservative Baptist Quarterly* (Summer, 1958).

14. Robert Lightner, *Neo-evangelicalism* (Findlay, Ohio: Dunham Publishing Co., n.d.), p. 8.

15. William Hordern, *A Layman's Guide to Protestant Theology* (New York: The Macmillan Company, 1955), pp. 67-68; *The Case for a New Reformation Theology* (Philadelphia: The Westminster Press, 1959), pp. 15-16; *New Directions in Theology Today: Volume I Introduction* (Philadelphia: The Westminster Press, 1966), chapter 4.

16. Edward Carnell, "Post-Fundamentalist Faith," *Christian Century*, LXXVI, No. 34 (Aug. 26, 1959), p. 271.

17. Advertisement by University of Chicago Divinity School in *Christianity Today*, Vol. VI, No. 14 (April 13, 1962), p. 271.

18. "Fundamentalist Revival," *Christian Century*, Vol. LXXIV, No. 25 (June 19, 1957), pp. 749-51.

19. "Demythologizing Neoevangelicalism," *Christian Century*, LXXXII, No. 37 (Sept. 15, 1965), pp. 1115-16.

20. "How About That?" *Christian Century*, Vol. LXXXIV, No. 26 (June 28, 1967), pp. 16-19.

21. George Ladd, *The New Testament and Criticism* (Grand Rapids: Wm. B. Eerdmans Publishing Co., 1967).

22. Bernard Ramm, *Special Revelation and the Word of God* (Grand Rapids: Wm. B. Eerdmans Publishing Co., 1961), p. 7.

23. Bernard Ramm, "The Most Critical Scientific Issue," *Christianity Today*, Vol. VII, No. 1 (October 12, 1962), p. 34.

24. Bernard Ramm, "Karl Barth and Analytic Philosophy," *Christian Century*, Vol. LXXXX, No. 15 (April 11, 1962), pp. 453-55.

Bibliography

Alexander, C. D., "The Failure of Evangelicalism," *Eternity* Vol. 4, No. 5 (May, 1953), pp. 7ff.

Alton, Everest, ed., *Modern Science and Christian Faith* (Wheaton, Ill.: Van Kampen Press, 1948).

Ashbrook, William A., "The New Evangelicalism—The New Neutralism," *Central Conservative Baptist Quarterly* (Summer, 1959).

Bass, Clarence, *Backgrounds to Dispensationalism* (Grand Rapids: Wm. B. Eerdmans Publishing Co., 1960).

Bayly, Joseph T., "The Christian View of Science and Scripture," *Eternity,* Vol. 6, No. 8 (August, 1955), pp. 4ff.

Bender, Thorwald W., "What's New in Theology?" *Bulletin of the Evangelical Theological Society,* Vol. 2, No. 3 (Summer, 1959).

Bible Champion, Vol. 32 (1926), pp. 503-04.

Blaiklock, E. M., "Conservatism, Liberalism and Neo-orthodoxy, a Present-day Survey," *Eternity,* Vol. 11, No. 8 (August, 1960), pp. 21ff.

Bouma, Clarence, "Orthodox Theological Scholarship," *Calvin Forum* (February, 1950), p. 134.

Bruce, F. F., "Criticism and Faith," *Christianity Today,* Vol. V, No. 4 (November 21, 1960), pp. 9-12.

Bryan, William Jennings, *Bryan's Last Word on Evolution* (Chicago: Bible Institute Colportage Press, n.d.).

——, *In His Image* (Westwood: Fleming H. Revell Company, 1922).

Buswell, James Oliver, Jr., "The Case for Orthodox Theology," *Bible Presbyterian Reporter,* Vol. IV, No. 10 (December, 1959), pp. 16-18.

Buswell, James Oliver, III, "A Creationist Interpretation of Prehistoric Man," *Evolution and Christian Thought Today,* Russell L. Mixter, ed. (Grand Rapids: Wm. B. Eerdmans Publishing Co., 1960), pp. 107-22.

Bullock, Wilbur L., "Systematics and Speculation," *Evolution and Christian Thought Today,* Russell L. Mixter, ed. (Grand Rapids: Wm. B. Eerdmans Publishing Co., 1960), pp. 107-22.

Bulletin of Fuller Theological Seminary, catalogue issue, Vol. VIII, No. 2 (March, 1958).

Carnell, Edward J., "Barth as Inconsistent Evangelical," *Christian Century,* Vol. LXXIX, No. 23 (June 6, 1962), pp. 713-14.

——, *The Burden of Soren Kierkegaard* (Grand Rapids: Wm. B. Eerdmans Publishing Co., 1965).

——, *The Case for Orthodox Theology* (Philadelphia: The Westminster Press, 1959).

——, "A Christian Social Ethics," *Christian Century,* Vol. LXXX, No. 32 (August 7, 1963), pp. 979-80.

——, "The Existence of God," *Moody Monthly,* Vol. 50, No. 5 (January, 1950), pp. 312ff.

——, "The Fear of Death," *Christian Century,* Vol. LXXX, No. 5 (January 30, 1963), pp. 136-37.

——, "Fundamentalism," *Handbook of Christian Theology,* Marvin Halverson, ed. (Cleveland: The World Publishing Company, 1965).

——, "The Government of the Church," *Basic Christian Doctrines,* Carl F. H. Henry, ed. (New York: Holt, Rinehart & Winston, Inc., 1962), pp. 248-54.

——, *An Introduction to Christian Apologetics* (Grand Rapids: Wm. B. Eerdmans Publishing Co., 1961).

——, *The Kingdom of Love and the Pride of Life* (Grand Rapids: Wm. B. Eerdmans Publishing Co., 1961).

——, "Niebuhr's Criterion of Verification," *Reinhold Niebuhr, His Religious, Social and Political Thought,* C. W. Kegley and R. W. Bretall, eds. (New York: The Macmillan Company, 1956).

——, "Orthodoxy: Cultic vs. Classical," *Christian Century,* Vol. LXXVII, No. 13 (March 30, 1960), pp. 377-79.

——, *A Philosophy of the Christian Religion* (Grand Rapids: Wm. B. Eerdmans Publishing Co., 1952).

——, "Post-Fundamentalist Faith," *Christian Century,* Vol. LXXVI, No. 34 (August 26, 1959), p. 971.

——, "The Problem of Religious Authority," *His,* Vol. 10, No. 5 (February, 1950), pp. 6 ff.

——, "The Providence of God," *Moody Monthly,* Vol. 50. No. 7 (March, 1950), pp. 460 ff.

——, "The Revelation of God," *Moody Monthly,* Vol. 50, No. 6 (February, 1950), pp. 384 ff.

——, *The Theology of Reinhold Niebuhr* (Grand Rapids: Wm. B. Eerdmans Publishing Co., 1951).

——, "The Virgin Birth of Christ," *Christianity Today,* Vol. IV, No. 5 (December 7, 1959), pp. 9-10.

Clark, Gordon H., "Apologetics," *Contemporary Evangelical Thought,* Carl F. H. Henry, ed. (New York: Chanel Press, 1957).

——, *Christian Philosophy of Education* (Grand Rapids: Wm. B. Eerdmans Publishing Co., 1946).

——, *Christian View of Men and Things* (Grand Rapids: Wm. B. Eerdmans Publishing Co., 1946).

——, "Language and Logic," *The Gordon Review,* Vol. III, No. 4 (December, 1957), pp. 141-50.

——, "Logic and Language," *The Gordon Review,* Vol. II, No. 1 (February, 1956), pp. 3-9.

——, *Religion, Reason, and Revelation* (Philadelphia: Presbyterian and Reformed Publishing Co., 1960).

——, "Special Divine Revelation as Rational," *Revelation and the Bible,* Carl F. H. Henry, ed. (Grand Rapids: Baker Book House, 1958), pp. 25-41.

———, "Special Report: Encountering Barth in Chicago," *Christianity Today,* Vol. VI, No. 16 (May 11, 1962), pp. 35-36.

———, *Thales to Dewey* (Boston: Houghton Mifflin Company, 1957).

———, "The Bible as Truth," *Bibliotheca Sacra,* Vol. 114, No. 454 (April, 1957), pp. 4-10.

Clearwaters, Richard V., "The Double Divisiveness of the New Evangelicalism," *North Star Baptist,* Vol. XXXI, No. 12 (December, 1957), pp. 4-10.

Cobb, John B., Jr., "A Panorama of Theologies," *Interpretation,* Vol. XIV, No. 1 (January, 1960), pp. 94-96.

Cole, Steward G., *The History of Fundamentalism* (New York: Richard R. Smith, Inc., 1931).

"Conservative Baptist Cross Currents in Colorado," *Baptist Missionary-Evangelist,* Vol. XVII, No. 5 (May, 1962), pp. 1-10.

Curtis, Richard K., "Language and Theology, Some Basic Considerations," *The Gordon Review,* Vol. I, No. 3 (September, 1955), pp. 97-109.

———, "Language and Theology—II," *The Gordon Review,* Vol. II, No. 4 (December, 1956), pp. 149-51.

———, "Language and Theology—III," *The Gordon Review,* Vol. III, No. 1 (February, 1957), pp. 13-23.

———, "The New Evangelicalism" (unpublished paper), Bethel College and Seminary, St. Paul, Minn.

Dahlin, John, "Another Look at This New Evangelicalism," *Evangelical Beacon* (May 17, 1960).

"Demythologizing Neoevangelicalism," *Christian Century,* LXXXII, No. 37 (September 15, 1965), pp. 1115-16.

DeWolf, L. Harold, *The Case for Theology in Liberal Perspective* (Philadelphia: The Westminster Press, 1959).

"The Evangelical Undertow," *Time* (December 20, 1963).

"Evangelicals and Fundamentals," *Christianity Today,* Vol. I, No. 24 (September 16, 1957), pp. 20-21.

Feinberg, Charles L., et. al., "An Answer to Is Christianity Changing?" *The King's Business* (January, 1957).

——, ed., *The Fundamentals for Today* (Grand Rapids: Kregel Publications, 1958), 2 vol.

Ferm, Robert O., *Cooperative Evangelism* (Grand Rapids: Zondervan Publishing House, 1958).

Fosdick, Harry Emerson, "Shall the Fundamentalists Win?" A sermon preached at the First Presbyterian Church, New York, May 21, 1922. Printed by the First Presbyterian Church.

"Fundamentalist Revival," *Christian Century,* Vol. LXXIV, No. 25 (June 19, 1957), pp. 749-51.

Furniss, Norman F., *The Fundamentalist Controversy, 1918-1931* (New Haven: Yale University Press, 1954).

Gasper, Louis, *The Fundamentalist Movement* (The Hague: Mouton and Co., 1963).

Gedney, Edwin K., "Geology and the Bible," *Modern Science and Christian Faith* (Wheaton, Ill.: Van Kampen Press, 1950), pp. 23-57.

Graham, Billy, *Peace With God* (New York: Pocket Books, 1955).

"Graham in Greenville," *Christianity Today,* Vol. X, No. 13 (April 1, 1966), p. 44.

Grounds, Vernon, "Fundamentalism and Evangelicalism: Legitimate Labels or Illicit Labels?" (unpublished paper) Conservative Baptist Seminary, Denver, Colorado.

——, "Fundamentalism Needs a Reformation," *Eternity,* Vol. 12, No. 12 (December, 1961), pp. 21-29.

——, "The Nature of Evangelicalism," *Eternity,* Vol. 7, No. 2 (February, 1956), pp. 12ff.

——, "The Old Biblicism and the New," (unpublished paper) Conservative Baptist Seminary, Denver, Colorado.

——, "Study for Skeptics," *His,* Vol. 18, No. 7 (April, 1958), pp. 8-14.

Hackett, Stuart C., *The Resurrection of Theism* (Chicago: Moody Press, 1957).

Harrison, Everett F., "Criteria of Biblical Inerrancy," *Christianity Today,* Vol. II, No. 8 (January 20, 1958), pp. 16-18.

——, "The Phenomena of Scripture," *Revelation and the Bible,*

Carl F. H. Henry, ed. (Grand Rapids: Baker Book House, 1958), pp. 235-50.

——, "The New Testament," *Contemporary Evangelical Thought,* Carl F. H. Henry, ed. (Great Neck, N.Y.: Channel Press, 1957), pp. 41-66.

Hearn, Arnold W., "Fundamentalist Renascence," *Christian Century,* Vol. LXXV, No. 18 (April 30, 1958), pp. 528 ff.

Henry, Carl F. H., *Basic Christian Doctrines* (New York: Holt, Rinehart & Winston, Inc., 1962).

——, *Christian Faith and Modern Theology* (New York: Channel Press, 1964).

——, *Christian Personal Ethics* (Grand Rapids: Wm. B. Eerdmans Publishing Co., 1957).

——, *Contemporary Evangelical Thought* (Great Neck, N.Y.: Channel Press, 1957).

——, "Dare We Renew the Controversy?", *Christianity Today,* Vol. I, No. 19 (June 24, 1957), pp. 23ff.

——, "Divine Revelation and the Bible," *Inspiration and Interpretation,* John Walvoord, ed. (Grand Rapids: Wm. B. Eerdmans Publishing Co., 1951).

——, *The Drift of Western Thought* (Grand Rapids: Wm. B. Eerdmans Publishing Co., 1951).

——, *Evangelical Responsibility in Contemporary Theology* (Grand Rapids: Wm. B. Eerdmans Publishing Co., 1957).

——, "The Evangelical Thrust," *Christianity Today,* Vol. VI, No. 9 (February 2, 1962), pp. 28-29.

——, "Evangelicals and the Ecumenical Movement," *Moody Monthly,* Vol. 49, No. 9 (May, 1949), pp. 629 ff.

——, "Evangelicals and Ecumenism," *Christianity Today,* Vol. X, No. 17 (May 27, 1966), pp. 10-13.

——, *Fifty Years of Protestant Theology* (Boston: W. A. Wilde, 1959).

——, *Frontiers in Modern Theology* (Chicago: Moody Press, 1966).

——, *Giving a Reason for Our Hope* (Boston: W. A. Wilde, 1949).

——, "Has Anybody Seen 'Erape'?", *Christianity Today* Vol. IV, No. 8 (January 18, 1960), pp. 12-14.

——, *Jesus of Nazareth: Saviour and Lord* (Grand Rapids: Wm. B. Eerdmans Publishing Co., 1966).

——, "Man's Dilemma: Sin," *The Word for This Century*, M. C. Tenney, ed. (New York: Oxford University Press, Inc., 1949), pp. 3-20.

——, "The 'New Morality' and Premarital Sex," *Christianity Today*, Vol. IX, No. 20 (July 2, 1965), pp. 21-23.

——, "No Other Name," *Moody Monthly*, Vol. 48, No. 12 (August, 1948), pp. 866 ff.

——, *Notes on the Doctrine of God* (Boston: W. A. Wilde, 1948).

——, "Our Lord's Virgin Birth," *Christianity Today*, Vol. IV, No. 5 (December 7, 1959), pp. 20-22.

——, "Organizational Unity and Spiritual Union," *Moody Monthly*, Vol. 49, No. 11 (July, 1949), pp. 776 ff.

——, "Perils of Ecumenicity," *Christianity Today*, Vol. I, No. 2 (November 26, 1956), pp. 20-22.

——, *Personal Idealism and Strong's Theology* (Wheaton, Ill.: Van Kampen Press, 1951).

——, ed. "Principles of Christian Unity," *Christianity Today*, Vol. IX, No. 9 (January 29, 1965), p. 29.

——, *The Protestant Dilemma* (Grand Rapids: Wm. B. Eerdmans Publishing Co., 1949).

——, *Remaking the Modern Mind* (Grand Rapids: Wm. B. Eerdmans Publishing Co., 1948).

——, "Science and Religion," *Contemporary Evangelical Thought*, Carl F. H. Henry, ed. (Great Neck, N.Y.: Channel Press, 1957), pp. 245-82.

——, "The State in Welfare Work," *Christianity Today*, Vol. IV, No. 8 (January 18, 1960), pp. 21-23.

——, "Theology and Evolution," *Evolution and Christian Thought Today*, Russell L. Mixter, ed. (Grand Rapids: Wm. B. Eerdmans Publishing Co., 1947).

——, *The Uneasy Conscience of Modern Fundamentalism*

(Grand Rapids: Wm. B. Eerdmans Publishing Co., 1947).

——, "What Is This Fundamentalism?", *United Evangelical Action,* Vol. 15, No. 10 (July 15, 1956), pp. 303-06.

——, "Why 'Christianity Today'?", *Christianity Today,* Vol. I, No. 1 (October 15, 1956), p. 21.

——, "Yea, Hath God Said. . .?", *Christianity Today,* Vol. VII (April 26, 1963), pp. 26ff.

Herrick, Genevieve Forbes and John Origen Herrick, *The Life of William Jennings Bryan* (Chicago: Buxton Publishing House, 1925).

High, Stanley, *Billy Graham* (New York: McGraw-Hill Book Company, 1956).

Hordern, William E., *The Case for a New Reformation Theology* (Philadelphia: The Westminster Press, 1959).

——, *A Layman's Guide to Protestant Theology* (New York: The Macmillan Company, 1955).

——, *New Directions in Theology Today, Volume I, Introduction* (Philadelphia: The Westminster Press, 1966).

"How About That?" *Christian Century,* Vol. LXXXIV, No. 26 (June 28, 1967), p. 828.

"Is Evangelical Theology Changing?", *Christian Life,* XVII, No. 11 (March, 1956), pp. 16-19.

Jellema, Dirk, "Ethics," *Contemporary Evangelical Thought* (Great Neck, N.Y.: Channel Press, 1957).

Jewett, Paul K., "Biblical Authority, a Crucial Issue in Protestantism," *United Evangelical Action,* Vol. VII, No. 5 (May 1, 1953), p. 31.

——, "Emil Brunner and the Bible," *Christianity Today,* Vol. I, No. 8 (January 21, 1957), pp. 7-9.

——, "Revelation as Historical and Personal," *Revelation and the Bible,* Carl F. H. Henry, ed. (Grand Rapids: Baker Book House, 1958), pp. 43-57.

——, "What's Right About Existentialism?", *His,* Vol. 19, No. 1 (October, 1958), pp. 29-35.

Ketcham, Robert T., "A New Peril in Our Last Days" (mimeographed, Chicago: General Association of Regular Baptist Churches).

Key, Thomas D. S., "The Influence of Darwin on Biology," *Evolution and Christian Thought Today,* Russell L. Mixter, ed. (Grand Rapids: Wm. B. Eerdmans Publishing Co., 1960), pp. 11-32.

Kik, Marcellus J., *Ecumenism and the Evangelical* (Philadelphia: Presbyterian and Reformed Publishing Co., 1958).

Ladd, George, *The Blessed Hope* (Grand Rapids: Wm. B. Eerdmans Publishing Co., 1956).

——, *Crucial Questions About the Kingdom of God* (Grand Rapids: Wm. B. Eerdmans Publishing Co., 1959).

——, "The Lord's Return," *His,* Vol. 21, No. 7 (April, 1961), pp. 9 ff.

——, *The New Testament and Criticism* (Grand Rapids: Wm. B. Eerdmans Publishing Co., 1967).

La Sor, William S., "Beyond Biblical Criticism," *His,* Vol. 15, No. 7 (April, 1955), pp. 5 ff.

Lightner, Robert P., *Neo-evangelicalism* (Findlay, Ohio: Dunham Publishing Co., 1962).

——, *The Saviour and the Scriptures* (Philadelphia: Presbyterian and Reformed Publishing Co., 1966).

Lindsell, Harold, "Carnell on Scripture," *Christianity Today,* Vol. VI, No. 8 (June 8, 1967), pp. 19-20.

——, "A Historian Looks at Inerrancy," *Bulletin of the Evangelical Theological Society,* Vol. 8, No. 1 (Winter, 1965), pp. 3-12.

Machen, J. Gresham, *Christianity and Liberalism* (New York: The Macmillan Company, 1923).

Martin, Walter R., "Love, Doctrine and Fellowship," *Eternity,* Vol. 11, No. 11 (November, 1960), pp. 20 ff.

Mayo, Bernard, *Ethics and the Moral Life* (London: Macmillan and Co. Ltd., 1958).

McCullough, Paul E., "Shall We Surrender the Term Fundamentalism?" *Baptist Bulletin* (February, 1958), pp. 10 ff.

McIntyre, Carl, "The New Evangelicalism," *Christian Beacon* (January 9, 1958).

Mickelsen, Berkeley, *Interpreting the Bible* (Grand Rapids: Wm. B. Eerdmans Publishing Co., 1963).

Moberg, David, *Inasmuch* (Grand Rapids: Wm. B. Eerdmans Publishing Co., 1965).

Mounce, Robert H., "Clues to Understanding Biblical Accuracy," *Eternity,* Vol. 17, No. 6 (June, 1966), pp. 16-18.

——, *The Essential Nature of New Testament Preaching* (Grand Rapids: Wm. B. Eerdmans Publishing Co., 1960).

Murch, James DeForest, *Co-operation Without Compromise* (Grand Rapids: Wm. B. Eerdmans Publishing Co., 1956).

Nicole, Roger R., "A Note on 'Language and Theology,'" *The Gordon Review,* Vol. III, No. 2 (May, 1957), pp. 67-68.

——, "A Reply to 'Language and Theology,'" *The Gordon Review,* Vol. 1, No. 4 (December, 1955), pp. 143-51.

Nida, Eugene A., "Language, Culture, and Theology," *The Gordon Review,* Vol. III, No. 4 (December, 1957), pp. 151-67.

Ockenga, Harold, "The Key to the Solution of Your Intellectual Difficulties With Christianity," *Moody Monthly,* Vol. XLVI, No. 7 (March, 1946), pp. 411ff.

——, "Can Fundamentalism Win America?" *Christian Life and Times,* Vol. II, No. 6 (June, 1947), pp. 13-15.

——, "The New Evangelicalism," *The Park Street Spire* (February, 1958).

——, "Resurgent Evangelical Leadership," *Christianity Today,* Vol. 5, No. 1 (October 10, 1960).

Orr, James, *The Christian View of God and the World* (Grand Rapids: Wm. B. Eerdmans Publishing Co., 1954).

——, *God's Image in Man and Its Defacement in the Light of Modern Denials* (Grand Rapids: Wm. B. Eerdmans Publishing Co., 1948).

——, *Revelation and Inspiration* (New York: Charles Scribner's Sons, 1910).

——, "Science and the Christian Faith," *The Fundamentals,* Vol. IV (Chicago: Testimony Publishing House), pp. 91-114.

——, *The Virgin Birth of Christ* (New York: Charles Scribner's Sons, 1907).

——, *The Second Evangelical Awakening in America* (London: Marshall, Morgan and Scott, 1952).

Packer, J. I., *Fundamentalism and the Word of God* (Grand Rapids: Wm. B. Eerdmans Publishing Co., 1959).

Payne, J. Barton, "Hermeneutics as a Cloak for the Denial of Scripture," *Bulletin of the Evangelical Theological Society,* Vol. III, No. 4 (Fall, 1960), pp. 93-100.

Pickering, Ernest, "The Present Status of the New Evangelicalism," *Central Conservative Baptist Quarterly* (Fall, 1958, and Spring, 1959).

Pike, Kenneth, "Language and Meaning: Strange Dimension of Truth," *Christianity Today,* Vol. V, No. 16 (May 8, 1961), pp. 690-92.

Planck, Max, *Where is Science Going?* (New York: W. W. Norton and Company, Inc., 1932).

Ramm, Bernard, "The Apologetic of the Old Testament: The Basis of a Biblical and Christian Apologetic," *The Bulletin of the Evangelical Theological Society,* Vol. I, No. 4 (Fall, 1958), pp. 15-20.

——, "Authority and Scripture: II," *Christian Century,* Vol. LXXVIII, No. 9 (March 1, 1961), pp. 265-67.

——, "Are We Obscurantists?" *Christianity Today,* Vol. I, No. 10 (February 18, 1957), pp. 14-15.

——, "Born to Die," *His,* Vol. 13, No. 3 (December, 1952), pp. 1 ff.

——, "Christ, the Pre-eminent," *Eternity,* Vol. 15, No. 1 (January, 1964), pp. 13ff.

——, *The Christian View of Science and Scripture,* (Grand Rapids: Wm. B. Eerdmans Publishing Co., 1955).

——, "The Evidence of Prophecy and Miracle," *Revelation and the Bible,* Carl F. H. Henry, ed. (Grand Rapids: Baker Book House, 1958), pp. 251-63.

——, "God Tented Among Us," *His,* Vol. 25, No. 3 (December, 1964), pp. 1-4.

——, "Hand in Hand," *His,* Vol. 26, No. 2 (November, 1965), pp. 4-7.

——, "Human Philosophy vs. Jesus Christ," *Eternity,* Vol. 15, No. 3 (March, 1964), pp. 25ff.

——, "Hymn for Three Persons," *His,* Vol. 25, No. 7 (April, 1965), pp. 9-12.

——, "Is Doctor Henry Right? No!" *United Evangelical Action,* Vol. VI, No. 11 (July 15, 1947), pp. 5 ff.

——, "Jesus Christ, Hallmark of Orthodoxy," *Christianity Today,* Vol. III, No. 22 (August 3, 1959), pp. 9-11.

——, "Karl Barth and Analytic Philosophy," *Christian Century,* Vol. LXXXX, No. 15 (April 11, 1962), pp. 453-55.

——, "The Major Theses of Neo-Orthodoxy," *Eternity,* Vol. 8, No. 6 (June, 1957), pp. 18ff.

——, "The Most Critical Scientific Issue," *Christianity Today,* Vol. VII, No. 1 (October 12, 1962), pp. 33-34.

——, *The Pattern of Authority* (Grand Rapids: Wm. B. Eerdmans Publishing Co., 1957).

——, *Problems in Christian Apologetics* (Portland, Ore.: Western Baptist Theological Seminary, 1949).

——, *Protestant Biblical Interpretation* (Boston: W. A. Wilde, 1950).

——, *Protestant Christian Evidences* (Chicago: Moody Press, 1953).

——, "Scholarship or Piety," *His,* Vol. IV, No. 4 (January, 1950), pp. 31-32.

——, "Sideswipes and Sidesteps," *Eternity,* Vol. X, No. 9 (September, 1959), pp. 40-41.

——, "Sourcebook," *His,* Vol. 25, No. 2 (November, 1964), pp. 3 ff.

——, *Special Revelation and the Word of God* (Grand Rapids: Wm. B. Eerdmans Publishing Co., 1961).

——, "Steps to Redemption," *His,* Vol. 25, No. 8 (May, 1965), pp. 24-27.

——, *The Theological Reactions to the Theory of Evolution* (mimeographed, Bethel Theological Seminary Library, St. Paul, Minnesota, 1959).

——, *Types of Apologetic Systems* (Wheaton, Ill.: Van Kampen Press, 1953).

——, *Varieties of Christian Apologetics* (Grand Rapids: Baker Book House, 1961).

——, "Will All Men Be Finally Saved?" *Eternity,* Vol. 15, No. 8 (August, 1964), pp. 22 ff.

——, *The Witness of the Spirit* (Grand Rapids: Wm. B. Eerdmans Publishing Co., 1959).

Rian, Edward, *The Presbyterian Conflict* (Grand Rapids: Wm. B. Eerdmans Publishing Co., 1940).

Rimmer, Harry, *The Harmony of Science and Scripture* (Grand Rapids: Wm. B. Eerdmans Publishing Co., 1936).

Sanderson, John W., "Neo-Evangelicalism and its Critics," *Sunday School Times,* Vol. 103, No. 4 (January 28, 1961), pp. 74 ff.

——, "Fundamentalism and Its Critics," *Sunday School Times,* Vol. 103, No. 3 (January 21, 1961), pp. 58 ff.

——, "Fundamentalism and Neo-Evangelicalism—Whither?" *Sunday School Times,* Vol. 103, No. 5 (February 4, 1961), pp. 90 ff.

——, "Purity of Testimony—or Opportunity?" *Sunday School Times,* Vol. 103, No. 6 (February 11, 1961).

Smith, Henry Preserved, *Inspiration and Inerrancy: A History and a Defense* (Cincinnati: Robert Clarke and Co., 1893).

Stonehouse, Ned, *J. Gresham Machen* (Grand Rapids: Wm. B. Eerdmans Publishing Co., 1954).

Stott, John R. W., *Fundamentalism and Evangelism* (Grand Rapids: Wm. B. Eerdmans Publishing Co., 1959).

Taber, Marcius, "Fundamentalist Logic," *Christian Century* (July 3, 1957), pp. 817 ff.

Tenney, Merrill C., "Reversals of New Testament Criticism,"

Revelation and the Bible, Carl F. H. Henry, ed. (Grand Rapids: Baker Book House, 1958), pp. 351-67.

Thomson, G. S. S., "Death and the State of the Soul after Death," *Basic Christian Doctrines,* Carl F. H. Henry, ed. (New York: Holt, Rinehart, & Winston, Inc., 1962), pp. 269-75.

Tozer, A. W., "Can Fundamentalism Be Saved?" *Christian Life* (August, 1954), pp. 14 ff.

Van Til, Cornelius, *The Case for Calvinism* (Philadelphia: Presbyterian and Reformed Publishing Co., 1955).

——, *The Defense of the Faith* (Philadelphia: Presbyterian and Reformed Publishing Co., 1955).

——, "The New Evangelicalism" (unpublished paper).

Walvoord, John F., "What's Right About Fundamentalism?" *Eternity,* Vol. 8, No. 6 (June, 1957), pp. 6 ff.

Warfield, Benjamin B., *The Inspiration and Authority of the Bible* (London: Marshall, Morgan and Scott, 1951).

Woods, C. Stacey, "The Neutral Protestants," *Evangelical Action,* Vol. 19, No. 11 (January, 1961).

Young, G. Douglas, "What Is this New Evangelicalism?" *The Evangelical Beacon* (April 18, 1960).

Young, Edward J., *Thy Word Is Truth* (Grand Rapids: Wm. B. Eerdmans Publishing Co., 1957).

Young, Warren C., *A Christian Approach to Philosophy* (Wheaton, Ill.: Van Kampen Press, 1954).

——, "Is There a Christian Philosophy?" *Bulletin of the Evangelical Theological Society,* Vol. I, No. 4 (Fall, 1958), pp. 6-14.

——, "Whither Evangelicalism?" *Bulletin of the Evangelical Theological Society,* Vol. II, No. 1 (Winter, 1959), pp. 5-15.

Index